LOCKED IN:

A Soldier and Civilian's Struggle
with Invisible Wounds

Cover: When a patient enters a psychiatric ward, all possessions, including the laces from his or her shoes are removed and locked away. The laces and other items are considered dangerous and pose a possible threat to the patient or others on the ward.

Photo captured by my amazing friend and gifted photographer Marcia Seiler at **Marcia Seiler Photography**

LOCKED IN:

A Soldier and Civilian's Struggle with Invisible Wounds

Carolyn S. Furdek, PT, DPT, CPT(Retired)

ArdenPiper Publishing

In loving memory of my grandmother,
Eleanor Miles Steele Burkholder
(1915-2016)
Fill heaven with your roses.

CONTENTS

...'As we arrived at the forward operating base my commander was waiting at the gates. He gestured for me to step out of the vehicle and in a low voice he asked me for my weapon. I was done. I had failed. My career and my life as I knew it in my mind was over. I was locked in.'...

"Be the change you wish to see in this world" - Ghandi

PREFACE

I hesitated to put my story down on paper for over eleven years. My mother begged me since I returned from the desert to write a book sharing with others what few stories she heard from me over time. This is my attempt to finally share my war experiences, invisible wounds and the impact they had on my life. I battled for years with the misguided thought that soldiers should not talk about their struggles. There is a concept, at least in my mind, that one should not divulge the horrors of war. How could civilians, let alone family, understand? Soldiers should keep their memories inside, sweat and agonize in silence when they are awakened by their nightmares, and fear to go out in public for the shame or the chance that others might want to avoid us.

How wrong I was! I have spent many years in mandatory therapy, taking many different prescribed medications, and have been lucky enough to be surrounded with an unbelievable support network. Whether it was the therapy, the medication or the endless support (most likely all three) I'm now in a much better place. I wish to share my story with YOU, or anyone who may benefit from my experiences. I have accepted what happened to me as a consequence of war, my endless drive, my life, my personality. Some experiences in this short story, I have never told before. With the few that I shared with close friends or family over the years, I would get looks of sympathy and horror. I already moved past all the residual effects and they don't bother me to the extent that one would think. I sometimes think of these stories as just another adventure, somewhat humorous at the time. I was invincible.

I'm sure the stories I now share and the missions I remember are different than the accounts of soldiers in my units, the soldiers that slept on the cots next to me for over a year in the desert. People remember things differently. Everyone comes away with good and bad memories. Everyone's life is different. Also, not all the time spent in a foreign land at war is dreadful. I tried to share in this story the good times, the camaraderie fortified, the rewarding missions, and help we provided to grateful locals. Some stories I included are humorous, while others describe the unbelievable opportunities I was provided over these 46+ long months spent deployed or in-between deployments back at home. I believe all these events, all these stories contributed to the shaping of who I am today, to my invisible wounds, to my life.

While recalling my deployments and past events, I reached out to former commanders, soldiers, classmates and medical personnel to ensure that my memory and accounts of missions, terminology, and episodes were as close to truth and facts that we all could remember. Deployments and missions I lived through as much as fourteen years ago, I can remember as if it happened yesterday.

I quickly put this story to paper. It does feel good to get it out. Very cathartic. I share these memories not for attention, not for people to feel sorry for me, or for friends/leaders to apologize for some misguided belief that they were not there for me or unable to help me, but rather in hopes that it can enlighten the medical profession, complete strangers, leaders, soldiers, my friends and family, my support network, the very people that helped me survive and live each day as I struggle with this foreign state of mind. The medical community was as curious and confused as I was as to why this happened to me. They still are baffled by some of my stories and reactions.

I want those who struggle and those caring for them to know there is hope! I encourage medical professionals to share this case with their colleagues and students. Analyze my thoughts, events, symptoms, the ultimate diagnosis and debate them with your colleagues. See if any of your patients have shared similar experiences. Together with the medical community, let's bring this medical mystery and its proposed treatment, along with others' struggles to the forefront and continue with efforts to accept and help those who struggle mentally in America. Let's put this diagnosis, (the one you will learn about by the end of this story) the one that took over 10 years to uncover even though it is widely used in other countries around the world, in the Diagnostic and Statistical Manual for Mental Disorders (DSM) here in America. This guide by the American Psychiatric Association is the standard criteria physicians use to diagnose their patients who suffer from the invisible wounds.

This story is a very personal story to me, my family and my friends. I don't use full names and sometimes use nicknames to respect their privacy. I still work in the same hospitals I talk about. I visit the very psych wards to treat patients where I was once a patient eight years ago. I want this story, this medical enigma, this diagnosis, to open more doors and break down any remaining stigmas of mental health. I do regret what happened, however, it is my life and I've moved on. I've lived to fight another day.

Believe it or not, I would choose all the same schools, same career paths, same adventures and do it all over again. I've met some wonderful people along the way, lifelong friends, respected and dedicated leaders, physicians, and nurses. This journey of life has landed me with the best partner one could ask for and two beautiful boys I can watch grow and navigate their own struggles through this world. If I can make it out on the other side so can others. And many have before me, I'm sure. My hope is someone reading this story will come away knowing someone else, maybe even themselves, having faced their own struggles and can relate and benefit from these pages. As any good soldier knows, if you point out flaws in a system one should always have suggestions to make it better, and I have tried to offer these at the end of the story.

While I will never forget my memories, I will not let them dominate my life, nor will I ever give up my relentless pursuit for answers and further research to help others. Don't allow circumstances, however horrific and painful they may be, to imprison you. Take control of your recovery process. Reach out and seek help or let someone reach out to you. Let someone, anyone, in. If this story helps just one person with their struggles, then it will have served its purpose, it will have been worth it. Enjoy every moment as much as you can; Life has so much to offer.

PROLOGUE

The crackle on the comms radio was intercepting foreign chatter in the distance. The air was hot and dry. Dust on the ground managed to find its way into every crevice of my body, every bite of food I put in my mouth. It was now four months into my third deployment. It was the end of May, 2005. The interpreter with us was quickly relaying to me and four other soldiers in our vehicle that voices on the radio were discussing the approaching convoy of American soldiers carrying supplies to the northern forward operating base (FOB). The voice on the radio was counting the number of vehicles and soldiers in our convoy. The voice was demanding that his men must be ready and in position. I could feel the hair on the back of my neck rise and the muscles tense up throughout my body. We were in a deep valley. Our convoy had stopped to repair a broken vehicle. We were surrounded by mountains, caves, and rock formations which made it easy for the enemy to patiently wait, hide and set off remote controlled bombs hidden on the road ahead or mount a small-scale attack with the advantage of surrounding hills and quick egress routes.

We were sitting ducks, clearly at a disadvantage with our position. Lessons from the Academy, daily drills our unit performed prior to deployment, and battles lost in the history books warned about the dangers of these situations, the deadly outcomes they brought forth. Quickly we relayed the message of the intercepted radio chatter information to the other vehicles in our convoy. The mood in the HMMWV quickly changed from that of causal stories of family and sports to total silence with intense scans of the horizon. Methodical clicks of the safety levers on the weapons and the soft hum of the engines were all that could be heard for miles. After what seemed like hours our convoy slowly started moving again. Our eyes anxiously darted from piles of rocks on the dusty trails skirting our route to caves on the hillside deep in the valley surrounding our convoy. Just days before, an improvised explosive device (IED) had exploded and killed several soldiers from an American unit not far from our current position. The Taliban was notorious for repeating previous successful or unsuccessful attacks again and again in close proximity, sometimes using the same pile of rocks they used before to hide bombs that would wreak havoc on our convoys and missions.

This type of information was fresh in my mind due to my current position as our Engineer unit's Intelligence officer. I had purposely requested the non-traditional, often unwanted position for Engineer-trained officers. For those officers staying in the Engineer Regiment and making a career out of the Army, this position was often seen as a step down from a career path hopeful of earning stars. Rather, I saw it as a perfect opportunity to prepare for my future job in the FBI after finishing my commitment to the Army. I had already been through the lengthy vetting process earlier in the fall and had been given a report date for the training camp in Quantico for the summer of 2005. The Army had other plans for my summer, however. My discharge had been cut short three months before my commitment to the Army was over. I had been put on stop-loss with others in my unit, not allowed to be released from my obligation to the service. I was told my previous two deployments from 2002-2004 had made me too valuable of an asset for the Battalion's upcoming year long deployment to Afghanistan. They also needed to be fair to others who like me, were waiting to finish their commitment and leave the Army. The unit needed to have all ranks and positions filled to deploy. By this time in my life I was used to getting my plans for a certain career path changed at the last moment. Rather than get upset, I took my energy and knowledge of previous deployments and redirected it to teaching classes and setting up scenarios and drills similar to the one we found ourselves in at the moment. I wanted to prepare the fresh young soldiers going out on their first overseas mission. At the time I saw it as another mission, another adventure. I was young, careless, and invincible.

Once we were in country in Afghanistan in the Spring of 2005, I tried to make the most of my situation. I was able to learn new tactics, previous attack locations and the history of the region from several intelligence and combat units on our air base. Working with these units had brought ample opportunities to share information and further support my unit's missions, including building roads for local villages to access food, schools and much needed medical care. In addition to local support, we fortified and built new bases, airfields and outposts for our American soldiers spread across the region. I would spend my days in the Battalion's' Intelligence Shop, scanning all the sister units daily intelligence reports. I would visit the other compounds inside and outside the wire to talk face to face with their intelligence soldiers and leaders while also trying to prove I, the engineer officer, without any formal intelligence training, could understand the way the intelligence world operates. I even joined a special forces team at their compound and went on nightly security missions with permission from my superiors. My command was unaware of the extent of my participation in the missions or the respect I had obtained from these seasoned veterans. Later, a special forces commander informed me that one of my intel analysis reports had made the desk of the President's morning briefing. I didn't know whether to be intimidated or believe this was of any significance in the intelligence world.

Leading up to this convoy movement through the valley, I looked for any type of information that would help keep my unit safe. I wanted to know and understand the patterns and locations of past attacks and databases of previous fighters that were caught or released while living in our area of operations. My soldiers and I in our intelligence shop were always trying to 'connect the dots', understand the networks and patterns of the enemy. After four long months in country, my days were up to twenty hours long with no weekends to take a break. Although my commanders would often tell me I was doing way more than expected of a Battalion intelligence officer in an Engineer unit, I would always feel behind if I did not have the latest information to provide the companies outside the wire, to those who were exposed to the dangers every day. For months I fought hard to convince the other intelligence staff and their combat leaders on our base to recognize the value our information and projects provided to the overall mission. I often found the infantry soldiers saw their own mission (to hunt down, capture/kill the enemy) as the only way America and the world would win this war and the War on Terror. I eagerly shared with those willing to listen, the stories and information from the locals who came to us because we were building infrastructure vs. fighting with and detaining villagers thought to be hiding, cooperating, or assisting the enemy. Village elders would welcome our soldiers into their homes sharing with them the latest events and dangers. They would reveal the locations of strangers in the region. Children would sit and watch and cheer on our construction projects, eager to climb on and follow the big equipment around. Women trusted our female medics to provide them much needed health care. I believed these encounters were an opportunity to hear responses to America's efforts to help the Afghan people. Thus, defeating the Taliban. I remember a well-intentioned officer from an infantry unit sitting me down and trying to explain that we were just a support unit. We shouldn't be afraid or fear that the villagers or Taliban would attack us. His soldiers were leading the war efforts outside the wire every day. We were just there behind them, cleaning up and building better roads for the American soldiers and locals to travel. Later, we all realized how wrong his predictions were. There would be many attacks and lives lost from our own unit and units like ours over the years. The front lines of combat are often blurred.

Now, outside of the 'safety' of the base camp and deep in the valley, far from our outpost to the north, all my over-arching, nonconforming, confident, out of the box thinking to protect our soldiers seemed to be crumbling before my eyes. I realized that our vehicles could possibly be under attack by the very enemy I had read about and warned others about in my daily briefings. The attack I was told would never happen to us and I longed to prevent seemed imminent. Why would the villagers not support an effort that wanted to help them and help their children escape the enemy? Why would the enemy want to attack us? I couldn't comprehend or make sense if it. I believed, like others, the people welcomed our presence and help. I believed they wanted peace and prosperity for their family and their fellow countrymen.

One could easily pick-up on the panic in our interpreter's voice as he hurriedly tried to relay the commands of the voice on the radio and the foreign answers coming from each soldier as he acknowledged the orders. A lone foreign soldier sitting beside a shack with a AK-47 rifle in hand appeared in the distance. The soldier waved and had a big smile on his face. Cautiously the convoy approached the man and his shack and simultaneously we attempted to relay our position and situation to our higher headquarters at the FOB (Forward Operating Base) 30 miles away. We did not know if our unit picked up our radio traffic and heard our potentially dire situation. Communication through our radio was shoddy at best in this valley. We all knew we were pretty much on our own, miles from reinforcement and crucial MEDEVAC needs.

The convoy stopped again and our interpreter ran ahead to the soldier in the shack. From our vantage point in our vehicle, we could barely make out their conversation. We watched as they gestured to each other and hands waved wildly back and forth. Dozens of lasers from our rifles were trained on the chest of the smiling soldier. Our interpreter quickly ran back and explained that the soldier was a guard. There were several other guards posted throughout the valley to support us and help keep the villagers, our convoy, and our road construction project safe. He continued to explain their commander was trying to ensure his men were awake and in position to greet us as we arrived. A brief sigh of relief could be heard throughout the convoy but hardly a soldier relaxed after this encounter. Everyone seemed more keenly aware of the dangerous and sometimes deadly consequences of our mission. The mood was alert but somber as we arrived at our FOB.

As the convoy pulled into the outpost my mind suddenly began to race and wander into dark places it had never traversed before. Normally happy and outgoing, I became quiet and reserved. Prior to this convoy outside the wire, I thought I had finally started to change the infantry soldier's view of the 'support' soldier. Now I felt totally defeated. I had shown my inexperience. The communications team I was in charge of had falsely alerted the convoy and higher-ups across the battlefield to a threat that was non-existent. I wondered if I belonged outside of base-camp (even though I had been on countless missions in much more dangerous situations during my two previous deployments). I felt unworthy and ill-prepared. I suddenly feared all my efforts had led to increased unnecessary and dangerous fears for the soldiers. Hours before, I yearned to inform and share all incoming information with these soldiers. Suddenly, these new insecurities, paranoia, and self-doubt took over and I wanted to leave immediately. But, I knew that my presence had been requested and was eagerly anticipated by commanders in the field.

For months, I had begged and pleaded with units back at base camp for a special communications team. I had finally secured a much-sought after Special Operations Team - Alpha (SOD-A). They were an intelligence communications team that brought assets to the field that an engineer unit could only dream of at the time. The team I traveled with had high powered radio equipment that, once setup and operating, could reach remote base-camps, current construction locations, and the rear operating base with ease. The radios could pick up radio traffic throughout the valley. Jamming equipment, once in place, could intercept and halt enemy communications; thus preventing attacks and remote controlled IEDs from being set off. If pilots were put on notice, the communication team could secure drones above that were controlled by my team on the ground and flown by airmen back in the states. These drones had infra-red video equipment that could find the enemy hiding in the hills around us waiting to attack. The drones also carried weapon capabilities to knock out enemy positions pinning down our soldiers with gunfire. They also had fighter jets at their command, given fair enough warning, could perform flyovers meant to scare and scatter the enemy from their positions or drop bombs in seconds to clear the enemy out of their caves. The assets they brought to the table were invaluable. I wanted to show the foot soldiers that this equipment, in a small way, could support the safety and security of our soldiers often left very exposed in the difficult terrain moving slow construction equipment. But we could also provide actionable intelligence for the infantry soldiers to capture high value targets, enemy leaders and further support the broader international campaign. The missions from senior leaders, generals, and even the President of the United States to build roads, hospitals, schools; these efforts along with daily battles and deadly missions to root out the Taliban might ultimately win the hearts and minds of the Afghan people and win the war on Terror. But now, as my vehicle and team entered the FOB, I felt ashamed. For the first time in my life I froze and did not want to speak. It was like a light switch had gone off, I was 'locked-in'.

1

THE QUIET ONE

1978-2000

I believe that my childhood was unremarkable and normal for the most part. I was raised and surrounded by a loving family. My parents valued education, respect for others and a good work ethic. My family moved a handful of times around the country in support of my father's career but I was always able to adjust and make friends in each new environment.

At a young age I was drawn to the swimming pool. I found swimming refreshing and easy. My parents were always able to find a pool nearby and a team in each new state where I could continue to follow my dreams and eventually help provide me with many choices for college. Along with good academics and above average test scores, I had a good choice of swim programs in colleges across the country. One of my coaches told me, swimming helped me focus and develop my natural internal drive to succeed and complete a task. He believed that same focus ultimately helped me overcome many difficulties later in life.

Military service in my family was common but never expected. In fact, my mother often remarks she was completely blindsided when she heard I wanted to follow in her footsteps and serve in the military. Both of my grandfather's Buddy and Malcolm served during WWII. My father John and Uncle Bob served in the Air Force and my father's mother, Mary and my own served as nurses in the Army. My mother spent 29 years in the

Reserve and National Guard by the time she retired. My step-father, Doug, dedicated over 30 years of his life to the military. I always looked at their service in awe and knew at some point I wanted to serve. At that time in high school I did not know in what capacity I would participate in the Armed Forces but I did see it as an honorable way to serve my country.

When a letter arrived from a school called West Point my junior year in high school, I brought it to my mother and asked her why a military institution was recruiting me. In all my years of watching movies and exposure to TV, military academies were portrayed as boarding schools. They were institutions far away where parents sent their kids whom they could no longer control, who needed direction and discipline, or were simply kicked out of their local schools. Now they were asking me to come and swim for their school. My mother quickly explained The United States Military Academy in West Point, NY was a very prestigious school where many leaders and successful men and women throughout the history of our nation had attended. The vetting process to get in was tough, and up to a quarter of each class fails to graduate, but I had never been one to turn down a challenge.

After several uninspiring visits to colleges and their swim programs, where I was told to select ROTC or swimming but I could not do both, another where the coach called my mother worried about how shy and reserved I appeared and worried about me 'fitting-in' with his team, and a final visit where my sponsor freshman had to study for exams and left me in a basement team room under the pool with nothing but Colin Powell's book on the Army, I decided the Military Academy was the best choice for my career and my future beyond the sport of swimming.

The man in the red sash on my first day at the Academy greeted me shrewdly and curtly. As I stood at attention in front of him, with knee high black socks, black dress shoes that were forming blisters on my feet, sweat beading down my forehead, and stumbling over my words, I yearned for my simple life back in Georgia.

I had been so quick to dismiss my mother's tears at the drop-off point that morning. I was free of my parents rules, fearless, on a new adventure, and I was living away from home for the first time. Now as I stood there, I was trying to remember my father's advice to view all the yelling and criticism from the upperclassman as a game meant to make me withstand pressure, and shape me into the future officer that would ask tough questions and intelligently and fearlessly lead my soldiers into battle. My first night at the Academy I hardly slept. On the top bunk, in my training clothes I would wear at morning formation I tossed and turned all night. I laid on top of my crisp, tightly made bed that would mean less work to get ready the next day. I stared at the ceiling and questioned whether I would ever make it to graduation day four long years away, let alone survive the rest of the week.

I somehow completed the rigorous summer training and met some great mentors and classmates along the way who would eventually become lifelong friends, part of my wedding, godparents, and endless support networks.

As the academic year began, we looked towards our future majors and studies. During middle and high school I wanted to be a doctor. My mother was a nurse at the local hospital. I was a volunteer during my summers and when I wasn't working, I would jump at every chance to shadow doctors on rounds, in their offices or in the operating room. Even better, I was told if I wanted to be a doctor, the Army would pay for me to attend medical school. However, early on in my freshman year of college, I quickly learned my hopes and dreams of medical school were slim to none. At the time, only a handful of graduates a year from the Academy were allowed to delay entrance into the service and go to medical school. Those slots were reserved for the top graduates in the class, the best of the best. Knowing my almost insurmountable odds, I instead chose history as a major, and mechanical engineering as my required engineering track, only to change my studies later to pre-law and civil engineering before graduation.

The daily schedule was brutal at the Academy juggling swimming, academic and military duties and responsibilities. Swimming was my only reprieve during the long bitter cold winters. Yet, trying to balance the demands and requirements of

Academy life drained all energy for my time in the pool. Having set several Academy and conference records my freshman year, injury and other commitments kept me from advancing my swimming career any further.

While high school academics easily earned me A's with dedicated studying and hard work, I often found myself floundering to keep up in college academics, struggling to maintain a passing grade in every class despite my best efforts. In the classroom, I was surrounded by geniuses. They said our class contained over 100 valedictorians from across the country. There were many cadets who scored perfect or near perfect scores on national testing. We had more than 700 high school sport captains and athletes. I shared the halls with several future Rhode Scholars, Truman Scholars, along with many others who would move on to Harvard, Stanford, Yale, MIT and other top tier schools around the world for graduate degrees, start their own successful businesses, or command their own battalions. Many of my classmates could teach the class I struggled to follow as well as write the books and tests that we took, which I often just squeaked by with a passing grade. I'll forever be grateful to my fellow company mates and swimmers for the late night cramming sessions before exams to keep up with so many classes. But I did finally manage to pass all but one class, Physics; one of my favorites. I retook the class between my sophomore and junior year, easily earning an A.

My summers at the Academy were a welcome break from the rigorous academic's I now drowned in. They were spent in military schools like airborne and scuba, and working with units in the real Army. No longer at the top with my academics and swimming capabilities, I turned my full attention to the military training. I felt the need to excel at something the Academy offered. During my third summer at the Academy, I had the opportunity to join a cavalry unit with Kiowa Scout helicopters in Europe. I was handed the controls of the helicopter several times, always with a veteran pilot at my side, and I loved soaring over the countryside. On the ground, I completed the annual spur ride with the unit, and 'earned my spurs.' These spurs were the culmination of a weeklong field exercise meant to test the physical and mental will of the cavalry soldier. I attended airborne school and graduated with honors, amazed they would reward me for falling out of a plane. I was amongst the first group of Academy cadets to attend the Naval Diving and Salvage School in Florida because at the time women were not allowed to attend the special forces Scuba School

After my sophomore year ended and hopes of medical school dismissed, I had my mind set on flying helicopters in the Army.

As if a foretaste of the unpredictability my life and career changes would be, one month prior to graduation and months after branches and bases were selected, I was told I could not be a helicopter pilot. The scoliosis in my back (which had NEVER given me a problem) was one degree greater than the Army allowed. With my dreams crushed, I had to choose my branch for the rest of my possible 20+ years in the Army, right then and there. Due to the late notice, arrangements had to be made immediately to accommodate my branch change and base selection. An Engineer officer happened to be in the room and told me to choose the corp. I reluctantly agreed and walked out of the room.

Most people who knew me when I was younger would say I was an introvert and very shy. In middle and high school I quietly threw myself into swimming, academics, avoided dances and parties, and hid from most guys. It took West Point and the Army, the leadership responsibilities and lessons learned, and the friends made over the years to bring me out of my shell, give me confidence and bring out the outgoing personality I have today. Amazingly, after four long years at the Academy and never knowing up until the last week if I would have a diploma in my tube, I walked across that stage on graduation day. I finally got the chance to throw my hat in the air and leave the Academy with my hard fought college degree to move out into the real world, the real Army.

2

YOU ARE IN THE ARMY NOW

2000-2002 / WEST COAST

After a brief stint at Fort Leonard Wood, MO for the Engineer officer's basic course, I had orders for my first duty assignment. Before we dispersed and left for our new units across the country and the world, I sat down to dinner with friends Jess and Jenn and my father. After listening to our humorous and 'dangerous' stories from life as a soldier in the field, my father chuckled and remarked that we appeared like little school girls pretending to play "war". My father wasn't trying to be disrespectful. His memories of his daughter were always as a little girl playing with dolls and swimming in the pool, clearly a tom-boy as I climbed trees and raced the boys on my bike, but I never ran around the yard with a toy gun chasing the enemy. Although very proud of his daughter having graduated from West Point and starting a new career in the military, he wasn't anticipating hearing us talk about war games.

When I arrived at my first duty assignment, my unit was a Combat Heavy Engineer Battalion (400+ soldier unit). This meant we had dozers, rollers and scrapers and many other large and small vehicles used to build roads and airfields. We had survey equipment to stake out foundations and airfields, toolboxes full of equipment to build houses, plumb toilets, and add electrical panels and light switches. We also trained with and carried M-16 rifles, 9mm pistols and lots of other weapons to practice bomb disposal, mine clearance and infantry style tactics because in the end, every soldier in the military was expected to perform as an infantry foot soldier. As a young Second Lieutenant (2LT) Platoon Leader I was responsible for 30 soldiers; most within 2-3 years of my age and a dozen of which were on average 10 years my senior. As a platoon leader I signed for and was therefore responsible for dozens of tools and construction vehicles used at the time for our peacetime missions. These missions were training plans or adaptations of potential combat missions tailored to benefit leaders, soldiers, the community or the installation. Projects included turning old railroad tracks into bike and walking paths, building soccer fields (which later would come in handy in Iraq), and rebuilding the trails at a local boy scout camp. The highlight for me was a trip to Fallon, Nevada to the Top Gun School (relocated and famous from the movie) where we built staging areas and storage units in the middle of the desert to store containers used as target practice by the fighter jets that constantly flew over and dove around us performing their own missions and training throughout the month-long deployment.

As platoon leaders, we took care of our soldiers, tried not to make too many mistakes, and tried to learn as much as possible from our Sergeants'. We spent our days working out in the mornings with our platoon, and observing and learning as much as possible about the mechanics of our equipment and tools throughout the weekdays and sometimes weekends. We practiced, drilled, and trained relentlessly to maintain our readiness and skills needed for peacetime missions but also for battle. While our training was intense, well planned and rewarding, none of us could have predicted how soon we would ever perform these missions on a real battlefield, let alone within the first year of my time in the Army. Our lives were about to change...forever.

On the morning of September 11th, 2001, I was in a grassy field getting ready to start a run with my fellow soldiers. It was a little after six AM pacific time. Tragically, the events on the east coast were just starting to unfold. There were rumors from soldiers arriving late to formation that a plane crashed into a building in New York City. In fact, my roommate, Kerry, was with her platoon (30+ soldiers) in New York at the time, building a training Academy for the police department. We did not think any more about it at the time, continuing to finish an hour long workout. After a brief shower and change of clothes, I sat with my fellow soldiers in the mess hall on base, all eyes glued to the TV, watching with the rest of the world as the horrible events unfolded. The next moment we were all called back to our units for briefings. We were ordered to perform bomb searches in every closet and car in our area and our soldiers were issued live rounds for their weapons and placed on the perimeter around our base that was now on lockdown. Rumors of additional bombs and threats to all American military bases ran rampant throughout the day. At this point we were all running on adrenaline, all of us believing we were going to war.

I was called to my commander's office later in the day. I was told they could not get in touch with Kerry and her platoon in NY. They thought I might have heard from her by now. As the evidence and horror of the day presented itself, all communication to the city was cut off. Cell towers were overloaded. We eventually learned, that since the platoon was ahead of the construction schedule, they decided to take the day off and travel into the city for some sightseeing. They had actually been stopped in traffic on a highway overpass in NYC and sat and watched the planes fly into the world trade center towers. The rest of their month was spent laying concrete pads to establish a crime scene lab to allow investigators to sift through debris from the towers. That night, after the towers had fallen, I arrived home late. My neighbor met me on my porch with a beer. He knew it had been a long day for me. He thanked me for my service and told me my life as a soldier and his as a civilian would never be the same.

CAROLYN FURDEK

3

PACK YOUR BAGS

2002 / AFGHANISTAN PREP and ARRIVAL

There were rumors of future deployments and units going to war rippling through the Battalion daily for the next several months. Books about desert combat missions, deployment plans, and war time construction were taken down from the shelves and dusted off. Young soldiers eagerly looked to the seasoned veterans in our units. These veterans had deployed to Bosnia or Kosovo and the Persian Gulf War. After my platoon leader duties were nearing the end in early 2002, I was told I would take my place as a staff officer at the Battalion headquarters performing administrative work and writing combat plans, all the while waiting for a position as a Company (125+ soldier unit) Executive Officer position to open. A staff position was not appealing to me at the time. Units around the world with orders to deploy were looking to fill their ranks to meet combat ready strengths. I asked for one of these individual deployment billets if one surfaced for an Engineer officer. I was told rarely do engineers, especially young LT's, get those sorts of orders. When my Battalion commander called me into his office in the February of 2002, the last thing on my mind was getting my wish. As luck would have it, the day before my meeting with my battalion commander, I was told I qualified for the Army triathlon team, a 6 member team that would compete against all the other services in the military. My battalion commander informed me all these plans would be put on hold for now. He informed me the next day I would be assigned to a unit in Europe, deploying to Afghanistan. I would be a staff engineer for a combat engineer Brigade. (1000+ soldier unit). Headquarters staff or not, I was excited to get my feet wet, go to war, and serve my country.

My mother fretted as I eagerly shared my exciting news. I reassured her I would be safe. I would be part of a rear staff, far behind the front lines, at most I would get a paper cut. Later my stepfather, Doug, said my mother wandered the house for days, losing cup after cup full of coffee in cabinets and under furniture as she shuffled around the house mindlessly, fearing my upcoming deployment. While soldiers are away from home fighting in a foreign land, I'm reminded it can sometimes be so much worse for loved ones left behind. Pacing the floors, never knowing if you are the next to get the knock on the door in the middle of the night with a soldier and chaplain telling you your soldier will never be coming home. Never letting your phone leave your side for fear you will miss one of the few precious short calls from your soldier that could happen at all hours, whenever they got a chance to break away from a mission to find a phone. Sometimes just the unknown can be the worst part of the long deployments for those left behind, staying strong for the kids who miss their parent, continuing to work, managing schedules, and maintaining the house by themselves as they worried about their partner so far away.

The next few weeks of March 2002 were spent going to warehouses around my stateside post to get desert gear, writing wills and advance directives, and going to medical appointments for checkups and vaccines for diseases that had long been eradicated in our 1st world country. Apparently, I was one of the first soldiers from my base to deploy to the War on Terror. The civilians in these warehouses, often retired Vietnam veterans, shook their heads in dismay at my seemingly careless and eager attitude towards the dangers awaiting me.

The time came to leave my home base. My household goods were boxed and packed up in a storage unit and all my affairs, including my will, appeared to be in order. With fresh desert uniforms and boots, I left my current post to start a month-long pre-deployment training camp on another post across the country. The camp was meant to educate our small group on all the recent security threats once we arrived in country and learn as much about the language, people, and conditions we were about to spend at least the next six months in. It was here I met up with another engineer LT, Jen, who was going to my same unit and we quickly bonded and became roommates for the next seven months of our tour together.

Our month long stateside training went by very fast. Before we knew it we boarded a C-5 cargo aircraft bound for Afghanistan in May of 2002. It was very surreal sitting on a combat plane as it flew tactically following a ground level flight path and jaw dropping ascents and descents onto makeshift landing strips. My travel mates on this flight made for a strange reality. Here I was, a female LT dressed in combat gear, a Kevlar helmet and body armor, holding my M-16 rifle, sitting on cargo netting and surrounded by an NFL cheerleading team brought in by the Uniformed Service Organization (USO) to cheer up the troops. The girls wore their very short, brightly colored revealing uniforms. Nothing makes one feel less like a woman when, here you are, dressed to kill (literally) with your hair pulled back, wearing camouflage instead of make-up and ready to go into battle while the soldier next to you is completely intoxicated by the gorgeous woman sprawled across his lap. On the other end of the spectrum, the soldier sitting across from me, ignoring the ladies attention was very quiet and somber, sitting alone at the end of the bench. He was returning to his unit after escorting home the body of his good friend...one of the first casualties of the war. Nothing shocks your system more than remembering you did sign on the dotted line to make the ultimate sacrifice for your country. No matter though, we were young at the time, and of course invincible.

Upon arrival to Afghanistan I found my rear staff engineer position was actually in the capital city with a lone Special Forces Civil Affairs unit that had been deployed to the region in early December of 2001. These were some of the first forces on the ground supporting very small combat units fighting and pushing street to street to gain ground and immediately start to rebuild the war-torn cities after the enemy strongholds were overrun. They were a unit with almost all senior officers with graduate and postgraduate degrees whose main mission was to teach and lead the Afghan people in setting up an effective government, schools, hospitals, and a sustainable food system along with international aid groups. These Civil Affairs soldiers from the Army Reserve were 'weekend warriors' who left their civilian jobs as doctors, teachers, professors, veterinarians, police officials, and political leaders to deploy to another country to perform and advise locals in their respective work for the Afghan people. These soldiers were seasoned veterans, having been on multiple little known deployments to Bosnia, Africa and other regions of the world performing these same missions off and on for over 20 years. The headquarters unit was small, less than 75 soldiers and stationed in Kabul, the capital of Afghanistan. The closest American combat unit besides a small military police security force that manned the perimeter of our compound, were in Bagram Airbase over an hour's drive away. The rest of the Civil Affairs Battalion was broken up into small 6-8 man teams spread throughout all the major towns across Afghanistan wherever a Special Forces team was living among the townspeople. These civil affairs teams worked alongside or followed behind the Special Forces missions in each village to rebuild and advise the local governments to sustain trade, law and order, commerce and food supplies after the Taliban, who often held power in these towns were either taken into captivity or run out of town.

An Afghan elder reminded me once, there is not an Afghan alive that knows anything other than war. They were born with weapons in their hands and have spent their lives fighting either for or against those wishing to squash all means of prosperity and societal advancement in the name of religion. Children caught in between never had the chance, especially girls, to go to school or learn to use anything other than the weapon they held in their hands. I wish my kids and others in America could walk the miles to new schools like most of the eager children I met in Afghanistan. After the Taliban was dismantled these kids flooded the classrooms and ran to the schools every day, yearning to learn reading, writing and arithmetic. I wish they could see the excitement in the children's faces as we built new schools for them. New opportunities to learn what they had missed for so many years.

Back on my compound in Kabul, I quickly learned life with this group of officers and a handful of support soldiers was very 'comfortable' for a combat zone. The unit had bought a row of houses on a city block and cordoned off the streets to make a small compound in the middle of the city. We had running (un-sanitized) water, beds with mattresses, lukewarm showers, internet connections, washers (not dryers), a microwave, and electricity. We even had small children living on our base and playing soccer with us. The children taught several of us the local language and we helped them master their English skills. We also had an outdoor pool (that remained empty despite my pleas).

Jen and I lived in a house with a French and British Colonel among others. There were several international military officers on our compound performing liaison roles for their countries and Embassies in support of the international mission. The French officer would bring fresh baguettes every morning from the French compound and the British officer secured a huge TV, satellite and cable for our rooftop deck at our house. Life was good. We would drive to our job sites in our Toyota four-runners and often wear civilian clothes with a police style bulletproof vest hidden underneath and our 9MM pistols in our back pockets or on police style holsters strapped to our hip or our leg. As civil affairs soldiers we wanted to blend into the population more than stand out as a security force. We would go on missions daily with one or two vehicles and up to four soldiers at a time to visit the local schools, hospitals, and other international bases across the town. This cavalier lifestyle may appear careless given today's tactical standards, but this was a time before IEDs were set on frequently traveled routes (popularized in the Iraq war) and for the most part the enemy in our region had moved out. Our main mission was to socialize and befriend the locals, gain their trust and help rebuild their fragile infrastructure. Most of the locals I met embraced us and constantly thanked us for our sacrifices and our efforts to help them and their families live a better life.

One of the Afghan boys I befriended was allowed to 'squat' in our compound after our forces had secured the field where he and his family had built a ramshackle 'house' after their home had been demolished by the Taliban. He lived with his mother and sister in the back lot of our compound. He would often talk about how at the age of 9 he had watched the Taliban slit his father's throat for assisting the Americans and not conforming to the religious demands of the Taliban. This young 11 year old said he was the 'man of the house'. He would sell cigarettes on the street to bring home money and food for his mother and sister who were too afraid to walk the streets or shop in the markets. He would always come around barefoot wearing shorts or thin pants and shirts or a simple robe, without a winter coat during the coldest days. The soldiers and I wrote back to our families and our hometowns. As a result, my cousin Betsey's children, as well as other children across America quickly held clothes drive at their elementary schools and sent the donated clothes to our units. It was like Christmas passing out these simple hand-me-down items to the children around the compound and at our construction sites. I was later told, my cousin's son, John Henry, was delighted when he saw a picture I forwarded back of a child wearing the very same coat he had worn the previous winter, now donated to this child in a foreign land. We always looked forward to seeing the little Afghan boy on our compound as he would come around in the morning. He joyfully chose a different shoe to wear from his vast collection he had now amassed from the generosity of the families back home. He would come around proudly showing off his new sneakers, flip flops, or pink jelly shoes. A different pair, sometimes mismatched, each day.

Children on our base camp who taught us the local Arabic language as we played soccer in the streets with them at night

Just some of the children who met us at our constructions sites each day as we constructed wells and new schools. The children always made the long hot days entertaining and reminded us why we were there

As an engineer assigned to the Civil Affairs unit, I had two responsibilities. The first was to manage construction projects with local Afghan contractors providing the laborers and supplies around the outskirts of the city to rebuild bombed out schools, veterinarian clinics and schools, and much needed wells for clean drinking water. The third world construction standards and tools used by the locals were far from those used in the states, or the high expectations of civil engineering and Army standards that we had used back home. Jen and I soon realized how to make do with what we had. Our goal was to help this country and its grateful people get back on its feet. The second job I held was managing basic engineering operations and maintenance of the compound on which 75-100 American and international soldiers called home for anywhere from six months to over a year. This meant I had to ensure the soldiers on my compound all had running water and electricity 24/7, among other things, and that the fortifications meant to keep us safe were in good repair and meeting the needs of the current threat situation. I always enjoyed watching our local electrician, Fareed, work around the compound. Fareed was a jack of all trades, and a MacGyver of sorts as he could fix anything and would quickly and efficiently work on live wires and connections in the houses, never allowing me to cut the power supply before he started. Appropriately, his hair always stood up on its ends. He would get shocked often but continue on never complaining, telling me it was part of the job.

I picked up the local language quickly from my Afghan soccer buddies and a young interpreter on the compound. I was able to hold the attention of most of the laborers and contractors, who were respectful of my efforts to learn their language and help manage their projects. They invited me to their homes and introduced me to their families. I learned about their joys and daily struggles. This was one of the most rewarding and eye-opening learning curves I was provided while I was on this first deployment.

Wood obviously was not picked up from a local hardware store.
Here a local prepares a tree limb for use on the construction site

A bridge under construction. Local construction standards and tools were much
different than most of us were accustomed to in the states.

Dealing with the locals was challenging but also very fulfilling. The men often did not 'work' with women. Women stayed in the home cooking meals and caring for children, and remained covered at all times in public. I was invited to dinner one night at a local's home and eagerly met his wife and children who were equally excited to meet and talk with me. The girls in the home begged for make-up from America, a precious commodity in their country. The young wife, very close to my age, was beautiful, ornately dressed and her head and face was uncovered inside her home. I asked her why she wore her burqa when she left the house and she told me she embraced it. She wanted to honor her husband and did not want other men to look at her or for other men to think she had interest in any other man other than her husband. She and her husband felt it protected her and kept her beauty to herself and her husband. Just as this young woman embraced her privacy, I met just as many young women at the Universities we were helping to rebuild who walked around the campus dressed like a regular American college student, courageously uncovered and embracing the western cultures and eagerly enjoying medical and political studies they were previously not allowed to study.

As an engineer project manager, I met daily with local engineers, leaders, school directors, and labors on the job site

The local laborers loved having their pictures taken with us, eagerly surrounded our digital cameras after the pictures were taken, and we were never allowed to leave without promising to return later with a printed copy of their photo.

Understandably, not every local welcomed our presence. Some led by fear of retaliation from the Taliban that still hid amongst them, attended secret meetings led by warlords who felt their power threatened by the American presence. The Taliban spoke out against the young women appearing in public without their covers and ignoring radical religious law. Now I, a foreign female, was a supervisor of some of these men and I was young. One day I stepped out of the basecamp to speak to one of the local contractors. We both, to our horror, saw a man who had stopped completely in his tracks, staring at this woman soldier standing before him. The man in the street dropped his pants and immediately started to masturbate when he saw me.

For every local who loathed our presence, I met and worked with 10 well educated and grateful Afghans who embraced our soldiers and the aide we brought to their country. One particular contractor whom I shall never forget and who taught me invaluable lessons throughout my time in country is Mr. S. Mr. S, had advanced engineer schooling in Germany and was fluent in 5 languages. He had quickly returned with his family to his country after the Taliban fled when the Americans arrived. He dedicated his efforts to his people and always quietly guided me in my engineering work with the locals. Mr. S once explained that his fellow countrymen and his country were broken. They were like an old man bedridden and sick from the last three decades of war. It would be very hard to expect them to jump out of bed and run around immediately after the Americans had freed the people from the oppressive Taliban. They desperately needed and were grateful for the freedom and international aid and were eager to climb out of that bed and gingerly start to 'walk' again, learn new skills, and enjoy their freedom again. After time, they would build their strength, lose the crutch of American and International aid that had graciously rushed to their side, and run their own country again. Mr. S asked me to help my fellow soldiers understand that we couldn't push the Taliban out and leave quickly; his country needed time to heal.

After what seemed like regular business hours afforded to us during the day, we were all provided much appreciated leisure time in the evenings. Sometimes I felt like I was living in a normal college town in North America. In the evenings when we were done with work and trying to pass the time, my peers and I would travel to other international compounds and embassies throughout the city. At one compound the guards were well known for throwing lavish parties. Whenever the ambassador at this compound was back in his home country, his guards would invite myself and several other soldiers to their pool parties with music, fresh pizza, and drinks. We would dance around in our swimsuits (something I never left at home on any of my deployments), surrounded by party decorations and Christmas lights, inside the safety of the high walls of the compound (just like college right?)

Life on this base in the middle of Afghanistan at this time was far from what I had imagined war would ever be. We would get the occasional attack of incoming mortars and suicide bombers and we would always respond appropriately. However, we were told the rockets usually used by the Taliban in our area consisted of a set of 5-6 old mortars from the Russian era, haphazardly propped up against a rock in the general direction of the target they intended to hit. When lit, if they were lucky, 1-2 would fire into the air. If they were really lucky, they would not explode in their hands as they set them up nor go straight up and come right back down on their own position. When a rocket did happen to land somewhere other than the location they were fired from, it often fizzled out in the air and would come tumbling down harmlessly to the ground, only to be found by a child later who would kick it around in the street like a soccer ball until sometimes life or limb would be lost when it exploded. One out of one hundred would actually hit the intended target and cause deadly and severe damage. In the early days of the deployment no one really paid attention to these 'firecrackers' that taunted us as they flew harmlessly over our compounds. I remember sitting chatting with my mother on a video chat when explosions could be heard around the outside of the compound one evening. I quickly closed the laptop computer screen, grabbed my body armor and Kevlar and walked to my assigned spot under the stairwell. With my role at that particular time only to take cover, I opened the computer up trying to pick the conversation back up with my mother who by this time was crying and scared to death, not knowing if I was in danger or would ever turn the computer back on. Once these rockets started causing damage around the city, we could turn on the TV and watch one of the 24 hour news networks from back in the states. Normally the media outlets could give enough information in order for the soldiers who didn't reside in the operations center, a general idea of what was under attack in the city. It all seemed like a wild west adventure to me and up until this time it was still 'fun'.

Driving in the streets of Afghanistan was a very dangerous and a challenging adventure in itself. The streets were filled with pedestrians, dogs, children playing, bicycles, carts, cars and trucks darting in and out of traffic without a sense of rules. As the driver I had a stick shift on my left and sat on the right side of the car. I had to harrowingly traverse the narrow roads and trails with cars speeding towards me on the right and sometimes on my left without a speed limit to follow. I once tried to make a left turn into the US Embassy on one of our weekly visits to their offices in the summer of 2002. A car behind me had decided I was taking too long and darted out on my left side (an unanticipated action) to go around me. Our bumpers harmlessly knocked into each other and the young Afghan came out yelling and screaming furious that I had dented his car. I learned he was the son of a local warlord and his father had later placed a 'bounty' on my head for my 'careless' actions towards his son. Nothing really came of this, but the fact that locals could have so much power over one another baffled me.

One day I was sent to the embassy to join a convoy with the American Ambassador as well as a dozen members of the Senate and Congress from Washington. My orders were to take them on a tour of a new school under construction. I was one of several in charge of managing the construction of the popular girl's school at the time. When I arrived, the secret service in charge of the congressional security detail told me to ride in the lead vehicle since I knew the route to the school, as I traversed it daily. As we were loading into the vehicles to head out, the lead guard of the detail said they were changing the route due to new security threats and threw a hastily drawn map on a napkin into my hands. I was responsible for leading this convoy of 9 large, black, foreign looking SUVs through the streets of Kabul out to my job site on a route I had never taken before. The age old adage 'can't spell LOST without LT' came into play and this young LT had the entire convoy doing circles around the streets time and time again until I finally managed to get us out to the job site. Once we arrived the politicians thanked me for the wonderful tour of the city I had provided. They were unaware of my poor sense of direction. The security detail just shook their heads. They had been screaming at me on the radio since I took the first wrong turn and told me I would be responsible for any and all attacks taken on our political leaders.

Luckily we were never attacked. Most of us never really believed at our compound, at the time, the locals would attack us. Our unit was not knocking down doors in the middle of the night or killing the enemy living and hiding amongst the people. While our combat troops had 'freed' the people in the city of the tight deadly grasp of the Taliban, we were the soldiers providing locals jobs with new skills, building schools for their children, and pumping much needed money back into the local economy.

Each and every day on this deployment I found myself on amazing adventures and unexpected opportunities. Often an American doctor on base (we called him Doc Hollywood) would leave the compound to visit and care for locals in the city. He came to me one day asking for help because force protection rules at the time required at least 2 soldiers to leave the compound together and one had to have a rifle. He asked me to come along to see a local patient and to bring an M4 carbine weapon. We headed down the block to the largest compound in the city at the time. We drove past all the local and American guards and literally up the steps and right into the front doors of a war torn palace with our car. At the top of the steps we turned and walked right into the bedroom of the King of Afghanistan, Mohammed Zahir Shah. The King shared the compound with the President of the country Hamid Karzai at the time. Much like England, the King was mostly a figurehead now and for the last three decades had spent his years in exile while the Taliban had taken over his country. Upon his return, with the Taliban constantly making attempts on his life, he lacked faith in his local countrymen and their medical training. He now looked towards Doc Hollywood to take care of his medical needs. The King had a great sense of humor and enjoyed the company of the Americans. His daughter interpreted for us as he shared an American soda, cracked jokes, showed us around the palace, and admired my M4 carbine.

I have so many stories like this one from my first deployment I'm still amazed at the opportunities I had and the people I got to meet and work with on a daily basis. However, for every funny, charming story, I also have the stories that remind me I was not on holidays or a vacation but rather in a country at war.

4

A LITTLE DICEY

2002 / AFGHANISTAN

In late August I had the chance to join a Special Forces team in another village. I was eager to get out of town and go deeper into the countryside, explore my surroundings and meet more locals. I happily jumped at the opportunity. I was given orders to go out and use my engineering skills to assist a remote unit in the hills of Afghanistan. The air-crew that performed the combat landing dropped me off in what looked like a deserted landing strip. Once the plane stopped, the crew was eager to get in the air and off the vulnerable airstrip surrounded by tall mountains and a known Taliban stronghold. I quickly jumped out along with a resupply for the team that had met me on the airstrip. Besides the couple of members dressed in local drab and part camouflage fatigues, a goat and an abandoned shack was all I could see around me. A tanned young bearded man, dressed like a local and carrying an AK-47 Soviet made rifle, introduced himself as the leader and Captain (CPT) of the 12 man US special forces team. He told me they had requested someone to come out and fix their generator. Somewhere along the lines the request for a mechanic had been lost and headquarters thought it best to send out the rookie engineer who turned the generator on and off at the base camp in Kabul. Without realizing it they sent a soldier who could barely figure out the TV let alone repair a generator, to address the problem. The CPT and I looked at each other blankly, he finally shrugged and said, "Well, the next resupply plane won't be back for another week so I guess you are coming home with me."

This unit lived in a much smaller space than my post back in Kabul. In order to survive they made their own rules, survived on mostly local food, and fought with and against the Taliban daily. By this I mean they would have meetings with the city elders and clerics during the day and at night fight off the sometimes deadly attacks (led by the same clerics) on their safe house in the middle of the city. Everyone on the compound took turns manning a one man position in shifts at all hours, including me while I was there. We watched over the compound as the rest slept, ate, and worked outside the house. We were ready to alert everyone if a bomb was thrown or an attempt to breach our wire was made.

Here I was, a woman, stepping into a remote village in the hills of Afghanistan, in a male dominated world. The news of my presence in the streets traveled fast. The sight of my exposed hair and face had started a riot amongst the local warlord and his people. They were unhappy that I was in public without a shawl to cover my face and head. The Special Forces (SF) guys, had always bent to their demands and tried to respect the local customs. At this point they were tired of making constant amends and refused to have me cover myself. I was quickly whisked away into the safety of the compound as the glass and rocks started to fly in my direction. Other than joining the occasional security mission to search the caves frequented by enemy fighters, or running the dozens of marble palace steps of the local warlord to maintain my fitness, my week was spent mostly in the bathroom. Eating the local food wreaks havoc on a foreigners stomach. The meat hung in the hot sun, swarming with flies all day. The locals and animals bathed and defecated in the same water used to drink, wash, and cook our meals. Just as important as the weapon at our side, strong antibiotics kept us safe and combat effective throughout our deployments. When I finally caught a flight back to Kabul, I was eager to return to my compound and mostly American food. My 'seat' on my return flight was a standing position between the pilots in the cockpit as we landed and took off from small American outposts located throughout the country. This position on a military aircraft performing nap-of-the-earth flying (a very low altitude flight course) in a combat zone has got to be better than any amusement park ride ever invented.

When I returned to Kabul in September of 2002, I quickly fell back into my normal routine. One day I joined a resupply convoy of food and water traveling to the Bagram Airbase. The airbase was nearly an hour's drive away. The soldiers needed help loading supplies, water bottles, boxes of food, etc. I was assigned rear security as my driver and I were the last vehicle in the convoy. Twenty minutes outside of Bagram my vehicle was stopped behind the local Afghan truck we brought with us to carry the supplies back to our home base. We were at the local warlord's security checkpoint, a place commonly used to demand tolls from locals for use of the road. Without good communication radios, the rest of the convoy did not realize we had stopped and my driver and I were quickly surrounded by no less than eight warlord soldiers, guns drawn and fingers on the trigger. Apparently the driver of the Afghan truck refused to pay the toll and refused the leader's demands to put one of his soldiers in the truck. The warlord's soldiers were furious with the blatant disrespect and now they were ready to fight the driver and the Americans apparently. By now we could see the convoy had stopped far in the distance. We all knew no amount of bullets from their position would protect my soldier and me at this moment in time. At this point I had every right (in my soldier's handbook), to use lethal force. I had heard these soldiers surrounding us did not have enough money for bullets but as I stared down the barrel of the rusty AK-47 rifle at the ready, I did not want to find out. The tensions were finally broken with the use of my very basic knowledge of the local language. Against protocol, but not against common sense, we agreed to take the warlord's soldier with us and we moved on our way. Two miles later we kicked the soldier out, never knowing his true intentions.

As my seven month tour in Afghanistan was nearing the end, rumors of another war in another country started to surface. I had the opportunity to extend my time in country, but my Battalion commander LTC F back at my post in America called and ordered my return home. He wanted me to return to my unit in America, and assume a position as a company executive officer. I was to use my experiences from this deployment to help take my state-side unit to war. I returned home just before Thanksgiving in the winter of 2002 eager to visit my family but also to prepare my new company for what awaited us in Iraq.

5

A DIFFERENT KIND OF WAR

2003 / IRAQ

If my deployment to Afghanistan was ever thought of as war, the deployment to Iraq would compare only as stepping into the gates of hell. From the moment our boots hit the ground at the end of February 2003, three short months after my return from Afghanistan, and weeks before our troops crossed the borders of Iraq, we were preparing for battle. Even with intense mission planning and heavily resourced supplies, there are always hiccups at the time of execution. As our aircraft was arriving on the tarmac in Kuwait, just like delayed civilian flights in the states, we waited hours on the hot landing strip for a stairwell to unload from the civilian aircraft. The tarmac was overloaded with aircraft bringing troops into the country from all over the world. Eventually, we loaded up on local buses to make our way to a remote camp where our 400+ battalion crammed into a handful of tents to grab supplies, pick up our equipment, and move out to our assigned place on the border. Comically, even our local bus driver carrying us to our new base camp got lost several times in the middle of the desert with no road signs or paved streets to guide us to the gates. We quickly realized upon our arrival supplies were limited or ruthlessly picked over as American troops assembled and prepared their convoys of equipment to cross into Iraq. Vehicles and containers we loaded on ships at our home base weeks before in America now arrived at the docks in Kuwait. Even though we had sent our own soldiers to accompany our equipment on the long trip over the high seas, our supplies arrived covered in sea salt and more than one vehicle arrived missing parts. Soldiers quickly scrambled to fix our vital equipment and locate missing parts in efforts to prepare for the upcoming border crossing in March of 2003.

The night before US forces cleared and crossed the border we were served lobster and steak. Make no mistake, while those of us without much rank would never know the actual date and time of the mission until hours before we actually crossed; each soldier knew with a meal like this, coincidental or not, battle was imminent. I was ordered to return to a rear base camp hours before the border crossing and pick up some supplies. At the counter of the supply tent I had to individually count and sign for among other things, over 100 body bags. A bag nearly for every soldier in my unit. This shit just got real! Long after the border mission, some of us learned the worst case scenario casualty rate for our company and the rest of the Battalion was expected to be as high as 75%. Our unit was manning specially equipped bulldozers that pushed down the berms at the border between Kuwait and Iraq. We anticipated heavy resistance on the border. Our equipment was used to push aside the mines and mounds of concertina wire placed by both the Kuwaitis and the Iraqis after the Persian Gulf War. Prior to deployment our unit trained with these type of dozers back in the United States. On our training runs we found that the mines that occasionally exploded as our equipment unearthed them were so powerful that the soldier driving the dozer could only take about two hits before he had to be replaced because the concussion from the blast rattled their very bones. The infantry units also used our Mine Clearing/Armor Protected (MCAP) dozers as cover as they followed behind our forward equipment, ready to engage the enemy on the other side.

Therefore, given our role at the border, the constant threat of chemical attacks and our subsequent missions to support front line combat forces, the worst-case scenario rendering our unit completely ineffective meant the overall war efforts for the entire armed forces, would agonizingly accept a loss of up to 105 soldiers in my company and still consider the overall mission a success. Thankfully, we were not aware of these numbers before the battle began.

The photographer captured the speech given by our commander in the middle of a sandstorm as we prepared to cross the border into Iraq

Soldiers from our unit taking shelter in bunkers with gas masks in the Kuwait camps as missiles fired over our heads

As our forces lined the border between Iraq and Kuwait, thousands of soldiers and vehicles could be seen in every direction. Our own dozers worked quickly to dismantle the berms and concertina wire to our front, as friendly artillery fired over our heads to deter any remaining attempts the enemy would make to disrupt our advance. Simultaneously, airborne and special forces soldiers were air-dropped across the country. What seemed like hours lasted minutes as our soldiers broke thru what was left of the Iraqi defense. We cleared dozens of lanes for the infantry and the rest of the American and international soldiers to safely pass and before we knew it the waiting was over, and we drove over the border of Iraq into a combat zone.

While not the MCAP dozers, here were some of our training runs with regular dozers practicing to clear and push down the Kuwaiti berms to support the 3rd Infantry Division's crossing. The actual mission took place in the dark.

Photographer: Cecil Webb

**All photos courtesy of our battalion's collection*

I longed for the days of Afghanistan, to be in a house with harmless firecrackers soaring above my head. A place where I could call and email my family almost daily. The days of working with the locals and children to rebuild their country was in my past. Now we wore our chemical suits, heavy body armor and gas masks for months as Saddam's missiles (thought to be filled with deadly chemicals and gas at the time) fired over our heads. We all hoped and prayed the charcoal lined suits and the filters and seals on our masks would prevent the deadly chemicals from destroying our bodies. We sat in our vehicles and foxholes around our perimeters waiting for the assumed resistance from the Iraqi soldiers that never really surfaced for my unit except in Baghdad and far north. I sat in a vehicle manning a radio one night and desperately tried to reassure an anxious soldier sobbing on my shoulder. I tried to calm him and convince him that he would again one day hold his wife in his arms and hug his children. Little did he know I privately wondered if I would ever see my parents and siblings again.

Make no mistake, with all the life-altering, heart-breaking, rewarding, and sometimes humorous aspects of war; no soldier takes his or her job or role in a combat zone lightly. Most soldiers experience firsthand the effect that war has on a country and its people. The soldier quickly realizes the control you hold with your weapon and the desperate pleas of help from the innocent victims seeking shelter amongst our forces. We see bombed out villages, homes and lives lost as the result of vital battles to root out the enemy or the enemy's attempt to destroy us. The restraint it takes is gut wrenching to not demolish the house where the bullets came from that took the life of your friend and comrade at your side for fear the enemy hides behind the innocent women and children inside. Or the blind eye one must take to the actions of the enemy in or to provide medical aid to the soldier that just suffered wounds after he tried to take your life. While I cannot speak for others, I believe most soldiers would give anything to return home to the safety and security of their family. However we continued to serve, determined to protect the locals and to keep the war from ever hitting the shores and streets where our own families lived.

Calls and letters from home were months apart. We lived in our vehicles or on the ground for weeks as we pushed North. All our food came from preserved meals ready to eat (MRE's). We had the occasional hot chow when the forward progress on the battlefield slowed long enough for talented cooks in our unit to set up the food trailer and prepare a meal for us. We were reminded daily that we were in a foreign land at war. Morning reports of support soldiers, just like us, killed and captured north and south of our position filled our briefings. All sense of time and the locations and missions our unit performed during these early months were hard to keep track of and remember today. After we crossed the border into Iraq we drove up a highway which looked as if it came right out of a major American city with green overpass signs and white lines marking lanes on concrete and asphalt paved roads. The only difference being, the lanes of these highways were deserted and the shoulders were filled with burning Iraqi tanks and vehicles all along the route. In the evenings we would leave the main highways and drive in blackout conditions on dusty trails. All lights were turned off, even a flashlight and the relentless dust storms would destroy all sense of direction.

Again, battle is always well planned chaos, at least this one was for me at that moment. This time our convoy (which I was not leading at the time), had gotten so far forward in dust storms and pitch black conditions that we had tanks and soldiers come up from our rear firing to our front during the battle of A-Samawah. Realizing our vulnerability and error we quickly stopped and watched them go past, and then rejoined the long line of support vehicles that followed the forward units as they pushed North. I had to go to the bathroom very badly at one point. I was alone in the front seat of a truck with one of my male soldiers driving. There was no time to stop and nowhere to hide in the wide open desert. Reluctantly, I had to cut a water bottle in half, apologize to my soldier, pull down my pants and just go! I quickly learned this is not as easy as the male soldiers make it look, especially sitting in a bucket seat and a moving vehicle. All modesty was long lost.

After crossing the border into Iraq my company was attached to a helicopter unit supporting the American forces as they entered and pushed through Baghdad. We slept in a perimeter we built in a farmer's field at night and the platoons built landing pads for the attack helicopters and medivac helicopters attempting to land in dust-out conditions. At one point, soldiers from our company and others in our Battalion built a hasty C-130 landing strip out in a field so a much needed MEDEVAC flight could bring out the critically wounded soldiers fighting a few miles ahead in Baghdad. We all felt accomplished as we watched the first plane in country land within hours of the start of construction. Critically wounded were lined up on stretchers waiting to load. I don't know what I expected to see as the airmen unloaded the plane with some supplies for the front lines. The last thing I expected to see was a John Deere gator driving off the plane along with an Air Force Sergeant carrying a wall mounted air conditioner. (An item considered a luxury our soldiers would not see until eight months into the war, sweating it out in the stifling 115 degree heat) I'm sure these supplies had an important purpose but there was no need for us to know the reason at the time.

While the main part of our company built airstrips and landing pads, some of our dozers and soldiers were called to support efforts further northeast with the infantry units. The bulldozers driven by our engineers were used in the city to push the burning shells of cars out of the streets and provide cover for the infantry from the resistance, shooting rockets and bullets as they went door to door attempting to take control of the city of Baghdad. As many battles loomed to our front we also were under constant threat in our own positions. Daily missions reminded our troops there were no front lines in this war. Early on, one of the Apache Helicopter units our company supported was rendered combat ineffective by passing over enemy anti-aircraft weapons in Karbala on a mission to Baghdad. The unit lost so many helicopters and flight crews to death or injury we all witnessed "shell-shocked" soldiers for the first time. One pilot brought out by early MEDEVAC was shot in the arm and stomach and his helicopter was completely disabled, but he managed to land his craft with the rest of his crew in blinding dust storms. Today, I'm quick to challenge any civilian or veterans from past wars who question the role women play in combat today.

Our soldiers knocking down a building with the 101st Air Assault. The building housed Iraqi troops that attacked the 101st as they cleared a village...Per our Commander: 'once shots were fired, the 101st would "phone a friend" (our guys sitting on the outskirts of town) We'd roll in, they would surround the building and we'd doze it down.'

Loading and unloading the aircrafts on one of the first landing strips our units made in the middle of the desert during the war.

This doesn't show the 1st C-130 plane taking off in country on our runways but maybe the 2nd or 3rd.

Our constant movement and battle momentum meant we went weeks and months without showering. My first shower was in a farmer's irrigation well two, almost three, months into the war. The unsanitized water was constantly flowing into and out of a trough in his field. I was the last to use it after all the soldiers in my company had bathed. The water, no matter how dirty felt wonderful as it cleared away layers of dust and grime. Afterwards, I found that soldiers on guard duty nearby with their night vision goggles donned (as they should in the middle of the night) had turned around and watched me as I bathed instead of watching the perimeter in the other direction. Again, all modesty amongst my comrades was lost.

Sometime during this push through Baghdad and further north I was sent back to Kuwait in charge of a convoy of slow moving trucks and empty trailers to pick up additional equipment and supplies. We traversed across the war-ravaged countryside as best we could where tanks, vehicles and Iraqi base camps sat empty along the route. Due to security concerns we hardly used the interstate road network. We drove the same dusty trails where

American soldiers had been captured or had lost their lives. Imagine a map of the desert wide and open, a big blank canvas with hardly a landmark, building or road at times. Now try and find your way along that map and camel trail with only a few tire tracks in the sand to follow without getting lost. Global Positioning Systems (GPS) at the time were just starting to hit the civilian market and they were far from accurate. The Army GPS's were cumbersome, clunky, and in my mind very difficult to operate. I nor my soldiers could never load or locate checkpoints or maps effectively. Our best bet was to follow the sun and set our compass southeast towards Kuwait. I had a very attentive driver, SPC M, and after 1.5 days, (the fastest time yet for a convoy to make it back to the rear from our unit) our convoy of dusty, dirty, war-torn soldiers pulled into a mostly empty US military base in Kuwait! My soldiers eagerly headed for hot showers, fresh meals and the telephone trailers to call their families. Because we had traveled so fast and ahead of schedule, I told the soldiers they could take an extra day in the camp before we were expected to return north. Shortly after dismissal I found a clean pressed uniformed sergeant, who had clearly never traveled north, berating one of my soldiers for not wearing the required flip flops in the shower stalls. Basecamps in the rear always have more rules and try to enforce standard Army protocol and dress codes used stateside. It might have been one of the few times that I intervened between a well-meaning sergeant criticizing/correcting my soldier. My soldiers had just returned from weeks and months in a war zone, seeing and experiencing things a young mind should never have to see. They had not showered in months. They came to town with the clothes on their backs plus a few dirty, sand covered items in their ruck sacks. Flip flops were the last thing I asked my soldiers to pack for their mission.

Reporting back to my Battalion commander, LTC F, up north over the phone led to praises for our speed and safe travels but he ordered our immediate return so another convoy could be sent south for more supplies. I had just released my soldiers for the day and did not expect them back for another 18 hours. Unfortunately my commander was told a vehicle in our convoy had 'broke-down' at the base camp and would take at least a day to get the necessary parts to travel back north. As a result, my soldiers got to spend another day calling home, eating good food, and sleeping in an air-conditioned tent with a cot.

After 2-3 months my unit pushed through Baghdad and we settled north in Balad, an old Iraqi airbase with commercial length runways. The runways were full of craters wide enough and deep enough to cover a double decker bus from bombs dropped by our brothers in the sky during the first few days of the war. These tactics were used to keep the Iraqi fighter planes on the ground. Within 24 hours of arriving, our soldiers had a landing strip capable of withstanding landings and takeoffs of some of the larger military aircraft. We spent the rest of our yearlong deployment rebuilding the airfield to withstand more permanent air traffic, constructing amenities for our air base, building soccer fields for local kids, and building bridges in the surrounding communities.

Months after the war began and our soldiers started to settle on Balad Airfield, our commanders were occasionally called to Baghdad for meetings with generals returning from the front lines. The meetings were comprised of important battlefield updates and supply requests from commanders stationed throughout the country. I was invited to go on one of these trips. A chance to leave the wire again and visit one of Saddam's many palaces spread throughout his country, I eagerly joined the convoy. Outside the gates of Saddam's palace, local people lived in squalor. There were ramshackle houses built along raw sewage and trash covered streets. When we drove through the gates, we were shocked to see green grass, flower gardens, fountains, man-made lakes with docks, boats and moats around a giant palace. I sat on one of the many 'thrones' where Saddam had once sat in his elaborate buildings.

I slept on a cot surrounded by rare marble and statues made of gold. I met with some friends and got to go for a run in my Kevlar and body armor. I got to swim in one of the many pools on his compound and pick up some free snacks at a makeshift store soldiers had put together from anonymous care packages folks had shipped to "any soldier" from home. I also had the chance to shake hands and take pictures with Robin Williams. He along with others were a constant presence among the troops and offered much needed laughter and comic relief from the constant threat of our surroundings. Support from back home was greatly welcomed. Letters from school children back home came in such volume they would pass out hundreds of hand drawn cards weekly to soldiers in our units. I remember one such card had a picture of an American soldier shooting an Iraqi soldier and the child had written, "Thank you for killing the bad guys. You are my hero."

Over the course of our year-long deployment, our engineering skills had turned the post on Balad into a very comfortable military base. The skilled soldiers in the construction platoons had turned a bombed out airfield into a sustainable landing strip within the first 24 hours of our arrival and then spent the rest of the year laying concrete to upgrade the tarmac to withstand the heavy air traffic required to make it a major resupply base. Our soldiers built popular outhouses with toilet seats, and designed and plumbed make-shift showers that could hold water from old containers so a soldier could take a 1 min long shower (considered a luxury). An old pool was filled with water for swimming. We designed and built snack and supply stores filled with amenities from home, and even a movie tent where movies were screened for the troops before they were even available to the American public. Our platoons performed every type of engineer skill imaginable. Whether it be rebuilding soccer fields and stadiums in the communities to removing discarded mortars and live rounds abandoned by the Iraqis, to clearing the roads of improvised explosive devices set by the enemy, our soldiers practiced just about every engineering task known at the time.

An iconic photograph of our units' mission to build an airfield as planes landed on the runway found its way to the front pages of many engineer magazines back home

One of the many structures for housing and support our soldiers constructed over the course of our deployment

Our equipment and soldiers ran 24/7 inside and outside the compounds to both support the war effort and help the Iraqi people. Photographer: Richard Gash

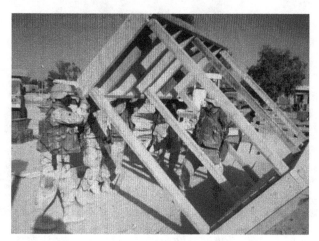

The frames of our infamous latrines with real toilet seats set over a 55 gallon drum cut in half. This was a hot commodity among all units in country until more permanent bathrooms arrived.

Route clearance missions performed to rid the roads of IEDs

Fields filled with munitions left by the Iraqis. Our troops cleared these abandoned ammunition stockades and often turned the areas into soccer fields for children

*Our soldiers constructed bridges made
out of abandoned tractor trailers and set
them across the moats in farmers' fields
for villagers and soldiers to cross*

After the fast-paced four months of 'excitement' with the border crossing, the push through the capital city of Baghdad, and our eventual settlement on Balad Air Base, the remaining days of our yearlong deployment dragged on ever so slowly and could only be compared to repetitive groundhog days over the course of our eight months remaining in country. I needed something to look forward to so I set some goals for my fitness and signed up for races to complete upon my return stateside. I signed up for an Ironman triathlon in California and one in Australia. Setting my sights high I also signed up for a marathon in Canada. After six months in country, I was afforded the opportunity to run and swim again on a regular basis in just a t-shirt, shorts, and weapon around the camp. Prior to this time, due to obvious security threats during the initial war efforts, we had to wear our bulletproof vests, Kevlar helmets, gas masks inside their holding case, and carry our weapon for all duties and activities including any short athletic workouts we happened to have. I could now swim in the pool on the base, ride the stationary bikes in the gym, and run around the perimeter of the airfield every morning when we didn't have an important mission to prepare for.

Our new battalion commander (who assumed command over the battalion four months into our deployment) was keen on maintaining the fitness of his leaders he commanded. One such memory that sticks out in my mind was an officer run he led when it was time for my peers and I to be promoted to captain. We were ordered to formation with our commander early one morning ready for a run and dressed in our gas masks, helmets, and body armor. Never knowing how long or how far his runs would last, we all thought we were done when we returned to headquarters after several grueling fast paced miles ran over the course of an hour in the 100+ degree heat. Upon our return to his sleeping quarters, LTC S quickly ducked away reportedly to drop something off in his room. Moments later he returned and quickly took off again, with orders only to follow and keep up. At this point we were dragging, but he seemed to run even faster as we trailed behind him. Once back at the showers, only minutes before our promotion ceremony our leader took off his mask to reveal for the 2nd half of our run we followed a young soldier from our unit. This soldier had the same height and build as our commander and looked no different with his gas mask and helmet on. Our commander, appearing around the corner grinning from ear to ear, asked us where we had gone. He said he returned from his room and my peers and I were nowhere to be found. We then had less than 5 minutes to shower, change and report to our promotion ceremony in front of the rest of the battalion.

It was also here that I had fulfilled my time as an XO for my engineer company. With my new Captain's rank I assumed the role of the Battalion's intelligence officer with orders to advise the commanders of threats to our soldiers safety and plan and lead humanitarian missions in our surrounding community. Six months after the start of the war, our soldiers regularly went out into the local towns for construction missions and the Iraqis and their children now greeted us with open arms. They were thankful for American and international efforts and the sacrifices our soldiers made leaving their families behind to help rebuild and protect the Iraqi people.

I was also starting to get very tired by this time, tired of missions, tired of the constant threats, tired of being away from my family, tired of the sometimes monotonous days of war. Being the only soldier in my unit and amongst most of the troops in country with back to back deployments, my commander and others around me recognized my fatigue and tried to reach out and comfort me as best they could. I was provided one of the few 'vacation' opportunities given to some of our soldiers in the Battalion after 8 months in country. I eagerly flew home to my grandmother, surprised her at her front door, and called my parents who were very jealous of my grandmother's guest. I tried to relax and not feel guilty for leaving soldiers who were not afforded the same opportunity and remained deployed throughout the year long mission in Iraq. I cherished these precious two weeks with family and re-filled my cup to return to my unit in the desert.

The remainder of my four months spent in Iraq consisted of daily intelligence briefings, and leading humanitarian missions to provide community service, money, and jobs for the locals in the surrounding villages. Myself and my soldiers in my intelligence shop were also tasked with collecting pictures, written accounts from soldiers, newspaper articles, declassified missions and digital maps of our locations throughout the war, and videos from our companies and their soldiers. All of these items were compiled into slideshows set to music and placed onto a DVD. A copy of the DVD was provided to each soldier upon their return home to America.

When our yearlong deployment came to an end in March of 2004 I was ready for a much needed and well deserved break. I had spent most of the last two years of my life living in less than desirable conditions. I had a weapon locked and loaded at my side at all hours. I had spent my mornings listening to briefings about IEDs and bullets injuring and killing soldiers the day before on the same roads we were traversing the next day. Soldiers on my intelligence team and I tried to plan routes to warn and keep our soldiers safe. I had gone to sleep at night with rockets 'whizzing' over my head, never knowing if we were the intended target. I could withstand temperatures as high as 130 degrees and freeze at night when the temperatures dropped to 95 degrees. I could sleep under any type of condition. The last 19 out of 22 months I had sometimes slept in full battle gear next to a generator that roared 24/7. I had led dozens of missions under constant deadly threats with many close calls. I had even run across a buried 'dud' IED that our vehicle drove over, exploded but simply covered us in a plume of dust and sand. I had spent my holidays away from my family and the comforts of home. I became hyper vigilant to my surroundings and always suspicious of lone piles of trash or well-meaning locals who worked with us and around us daily. One never knew what the intentions were of approaching vehicles; or if the farmer in the field was friendly. All too often we had reports of a "farmer" trying to break through the wire and blow himself up in our chow hall, or vehicles with women and men smiling inside were actually suicide bombers trying to blow themselves up in front of our gates. I was ready to hang up my hat, complete my commitment to the armed services and move on with my life.

With a little over a year remaining on my contract with the Army, I tried to settle in and enjoy the comforts of home. With back to back deployments I had learned to live out of suitcase. It was easier to put my belongings in storage than waste money paying rent in a house that sat empty during my trips to the desert. I moved over eight times in four years. Each time I'd clean house and sort through boxes of my belongings. I'd throw 'useless' items, clutter, and trinkets away. To this day, I still find myself not needing much. I don't care much for material things in life and spend most of my time cherishing my time with family and friends. Upon my return, I re-joined the triathlon community, trained with amazing athletes and competed in two Ironman triathlons and a marathon within four months of each other. I was in the best shape of my life. I qualified again and competed with the Army Triathlon team. All of this training was refreshing and led me to be in the best shape of my life. With new friends and a fresh outlook on life I knew my time in the Army had come to an end. I had always considered myself a career soldier since my time at the Academy. I now, surprisingly, wanted nothing more than a normal life. I wanted to settle down with the right guy, raise a family, and start a normal career. Somehow, in my mind the FBI was a normal career. Apparently a part of me still yearned for the life of danger and adventure however, this time I wanted to do it on American soil.

What seemed like twelve short months after returning from Iraq, in March of 2005 our Battalion received orders to return to the desert. This time my unit would deploy to Afghanistan for another year long tour of missions to build airfields, basecamps, and roads for soldiers and Afghan people.

Most of the soldiers in my units moved onto new units and posts across the country and world after our return from Iraq. These soldiers either planned to stay in and move up in the ranks, head to another military school or had at least another year in the Army to fulfill their own commitments to the armed services. A few of us chose to remain and fulfill the remainder of our short time left in the Army at our original posts with expectations that our unit would have at least another year stateside before being called for any additional deployments. Therefore, when the call came to return to the desert all of us were surprised our unit would return to combat so soon. All soldiers were "stop-loss" when the new orders arrived. This meant the Army and our unit needed the man-power to keep the ranks full thus myself and a handful of others were involuntarily extended beyond our contractual obligations. We could no longer leave the Army after our commitment was over. I was heading to my third deployment in four years. I would plan to spend the next year on the Battalion staff again in Afghanistan as the intelligence officer for a larger 500 soldier Combat Heavy Engineer Construction Battalion in the early months of 2005.

I've since learned that at least one peer made a case to my leaders to keep me home from the impending deployment, arguing that I needed a break. In my peer's opinion and that of others close to me, I had started to show signs of battle fatigue during the latter part of the Iraq war and that fatigue should be of concern to my leaders. While this fatigue was recognized no one, including myself, had lost confidence in my abilities or could predict what would happen to me on my last deployment. Little did I nor my peers suspect that this was the beginning of another battle looming within myself with an entirely unexpected enemy.

CAROLYN FURDEK

6

A FORWARD OPERATING BASE

EARLY SUMMER 2005 / AFGHANISTAN

Returning to the convoy mission described at the beginning of my story - My convoy with the special forces team pulled into basecamp...

The special forces team from my vehicle entering the camp looked very different from the engineer soldiers spread throughout the compound. They could wear long scruffy beards and grow their hair longer than other soldiers. Standard uniforms were often mixed with civilian clothes and SWAT style gear as these soldiers were living amongst Afghan people in their villages. They were gathering daily intel and holding meetings with village elders, instructing locals to run soldier training camps, leading advisory civil affairs boards, and capturing and sometimes killing high value targets. They were elite, seasoned combat soldiers, with many missions and deployments under their belts. They had confirmed kills with added skills many soldiers had only read about in books. Soldiers in the camp stopped what they were doing and stared, shocked they were under my command, somewhat in awe of this special team making their way to assigned tents and cots. It was unheard of and priceless to have these assets for our somewhat small construction mission.

Life at this outpost was very different from the large airfield basecamp. The smell of burning human feces permeated the air as barrels from the "out houses" were burned daily for sanitation. The 'comforts' of my 'rear' basecamp included washers and dryers, better food, daily mail and phone calls home, stores with snacks and sodas, hot running water, rows of trailers for sleeping, daily bathing, and bathrooms, even coffee shops and American fast food trailers could be found. Out here, on the other hand, soldiers appeared a bit more rugged and dirty. Occasionally they were provided with minute long showers using cold non-sanitized river water. Clothes were washed in buckets; their body armor was worn at all times. The bunkers were secured with sandbags and their substandard uniforms, not allowed at base camp, were worn out of necessity throughout this forward operating base. These lack-luster outpost conditions were actually considered luxuries to the infantry foot soldiers rucking across the dangerous rugged countryside alone in small units searching for and engaging the enemy on a daily basis and sleeping propped up against a wall or down in a hastily dug foxhole at night.

My anticipated Intel briefing with commanders in the outpost, (another reason I had been brought to the construction site), was to be held in the Battalions briefing tent. One commander brought his entire company of 140+ soldiers into the tent to listen. He felt it was critical to all the soldiers he led to understand the dangers around them. To remind them their intel provided the infantry and special forces valuable information as they sought out and killed the enemy. As I stood in front of these silent soldiers, watching my every move, my mind could not form the words. I mumbled and painfully stumbled over what should have been a very easy briefing. Why could I not speak of the past attacks in the area? Our soldiers needed to know the history and the dangers of the region as they advanced into the next phase of the road project. They needed to understand the networks of brothers, friends, young soldiers hiding among the innocent civilians who lived in fear of retribution from the Taliban. Why could I not warn them of the pictures of the dead bodies, the gunshot wounds to the face, the burned unrecognizable bodies of children in the villages that scrolled across my computer screen daily from the intel briefings I would gather from the units in my basecamp? Why could I not share the fact that some of those pictures were of the villagers that had collaborated with the Americans? Those victims who dangerously and courageously warned soldiers of strangers amongst them and their planned attacks on the Americans? The ones who had been castrated, eviscerated, eyes and tongues cut out, and hung out in the middle of their own villages as a reminder of what happens to traitors who help the Americans. Why could I not talk about the infantrymen and SF soldiers who were using the intel that soldiers at this FOB provided, to capture and sometimes kill high value targets? Here was my chance to tell them that everything they were doing was providing much needed infrastructure, as well as helping defeat the enemy. I needed to tell them if they didn't already realize it that the endless days pushing dirt and building infrastructure and roads for the Afghan people were much appreciated by the villagers and political leaders in Afghanistan. They were a vital asset contributing to the overall mission of the generals and the President. The lives lost. The birthdays and soccer games missed. The family celebrations and holidays not shared. The endless days away from their families, had all been worth it. They were making a lasting impact out here in this desert far from the luxuries back home and far from civilization.

The road construction project took our soldiers right into villages thru goat trails and gravel roads to provide locals easy access to the larger road network.

Photo by Claudia Crossland

The 117-kilometer road construction project was designed and constructed by our Battalion. This road was built to link towns and areas of the country to increase trade, medical care access, travel for elections and ease travel in general

These were pictures taken by a fallen soldier from our unit. Her family granted permission for the use of these photographs

As a Battalion staff officer I had easily held the attention and respect of soldiers, not to mention many Generals and members of congress. Yet at this time, my mind was elsewhere. What had I done? What had I gotten myself into? I had lost all confidence. Why would these young soldiers fresh out of high school and seasoned sergeants 20 years my senior want to listen to a staff officer, a cushy base camp dweller who had not been outside the wire on this deployment? Most of my time was spent inside the wire at the Battalion headquarters on the airbase since the Battalion arrived four months prior. Obviously I could not make it outside of the wire, everyone could see right through me. After 5 minutes I gave up and ran out of the tent. My sergeant, SFC V, ran after me, curious as to why I couldn't give a simple briefing and introduce the commo team and their assets. More importantly, he chased me down because I had left my M16 rifle. The weapon that never left my side even while I slept or used the restroom for the entire deployment. I had left my M16 haphazardly propped up on a wall next to the tent. A UCMJ offense punishable by a court martial or at least a sure fire ticket to stand in front of your Battalion commander for a less than desirable lecture. I ran away, straight to the 'safety' and 'privacy' of my sleeping quarters. My cot was surrounded by 20 other cots for soldiers both male and female. The rest of the night was spent staring at the ceiling of the tent, listening to the roar of the generators in the distance and the snores of the other soldiers around me. I was filled with self-doubt, guilt, fear. I did not sleep. I spent the night thinking about my impending doom with the upcoming mission the next morning. For once in my life, I could not find the positive in the situation. I could not "snap out of it". I felt like a captive being led to crucifixion. My mind would not stop racing nor relieve itself of these crazy, outrageous thoughts. The more I thought about it the crazier my conclusions would become. I also strongly felt I could tell NO ONE about them.

The next morning was a blur as the engines revved up. I quickly took my seat in the HMMWV with the communication team. Worry about my current condition could be seen on all of their faces. Their eager, confident leader was now speechless and extra baggage. They had seen my current state before with other beaten down seasoned soldiers in past missions from their units. It made everyone uncomfortable. In my mind their concerned faces were more like pity and disgust for me. Just another rookie staff officer that couldn't handle the expectations of a true soldier in combat. I just put my head down and tried not to talk. As the vehicles headed out the gate, I clutched my weapon as tight as I could, surrendering to the fact that I had lost my mind and any ability to lead. I felt like a private, one who needs constant supervision, ill-experienced and fearful of the unknown. I desperately watched the mountains surrounding us, determined to at least be a valuable member of the team, a soldier who could spot and shoot the enemy. I assured myself that once we returned from this mission, I would return to the battalion headquarters and never leave the basecamp again for fear of putting others at risk due to my poor excuse for a soldier.

7

JUST ANOTHER MISSION

SUMMER, 2005: 1 DAY AFTER ARRIVING AT THE FOB /AFGHANISTAN

What seemed like hours but really only about 30 minutes later, our vehicle came to a stop at the top of the mountain overlooking the current location of the construction equipment building the road. As planned soldiers in the vehicle started setting up their equipment, the interpreter tried again to understand radio chatter they intercepted. Given events of the previous day, no one was eager to jump the gun and alert the entire unit again to friendly guards trying to stay awake and get into their positions. After 7 hours sitting in the hot sun the chatter over the radio was nothing more than normal local guard banter, our own soldiers asking for breaks or directing equipment, and the occasional Afghan child playing on his father's CB radio. I remained silent the entire time. Mind racing, fearfully paranoid, recalling all my past deployments and heart stopping missions, I suffered in silence. How could I begin to even share my current thoughts, all of the past dangerous missions and deployments, or the loss of friends and soldiers that may or may not have affected my mental well-being over the years. My thoughts turned to my own family, my longing to be with them, to be anywhere but here. Eventually I realized one of the soldiers from the commo team was standing in front of me asking me a question. He wanted to return to the outpost. The construction work for the day was complete. Our much hyped mission was over. It had been an uneventful waste of the day, abuse of valuable resources, and these soldiers' expert and much needed skills and time. I had pulled these soldiers from what could have been very vital and dangerous missions with infantry or special operations soldiers sure to engage and take down the enemy.

Nothing to this effect was ever said to me by these soldiers. These were just my thoughts that I toiled with since the convoy arrived at the construction compound the previous day. In fact the team of communication soldiers had expressed a lot of interest for our mission before the trip. They were grateful for the chance to perform a new, unique, and different type of mission. They, like me, saw the value of intel my unit brought to the battlefield. We all hoped to bring back additional information that could lead us to the enemy. Connect more of the dots. They wanted actionable intel that led to capture of high value targets seeking to kill our soldiers daily. They believed this mission would provide that type of information. The soldier now asking me questions cautiously touched my arm. I suddenly looked at him in total fear. My mind was completely out of control at this point. I could not stop the ridiculous conclusions my mind was drawing from the current situation. I felt like I was a prisoner. I had failed them. Somehow, I believed my actions would let all these soldiers around me down, even my former professors as well as former classmates back at the Academy. For some reason, I believed all the lessons provided at the Academy, time and money spent swimming, and opportunities I had been provided throughout my life had been a waste. I had done something horribly wrong and now they were going to take me across the border to Pakistan and turn me over to the Taliban. This way I would never fail another soldier or put my unit in danger ever again.

I want to take a moment and go into a little more detail about my thought process during this episode. After my unit had received its orders for this deployment an old special forces sergeant participating in mock drills with my unit before we left on this 3rd deployment told tell me the Army was looking into forming a Special Operations Team that included women. They recognized the value women brought to the battlefield and missions in combat where they often encountered Afghan women that could not and would not talk freely to male American soldiers about the enemy or planned attacks that sometimes included members of their own family or fighters hiding out in their own homes. Often the women were not allowed to even speak to another man other than their own husbands. Americans therefore wanted to bring specially trained female soldiers that could be on the ground in the middle of towns and sometimes battles with the SF teams that could approach local women for more information. Afghan women were allowed to talk to and seek medical care from other women including women soldiers. The sergeant told me I would be a good asset to these teams and he wanted to pass my name along for consideration in the program. After filling out background information on myself and signing many documents, my application was passed onto the selection team for consideration. The soldier warned me sometimes evaluators would secretly observe me and grade my performance during missions with my Engineer unit. Whether the soldier was telling the truth or not I was now even more paranoid of my surroundings and the Special Forces teams I dealt with on a regular basis. The soldier also told me I could not speak of these types of teams and missions or of my consideration for the supposed classified program.

Returning to the mission at hand in Afghanistan in 2005, I wondered if the soldiers with me were a team of evaluators watching my actions in combat. But if these soldiers were really evaluators they never revealed their cover and the more I thought about it later the more I realized that they were regular soldiers, not evaluators, and I don't believe I was ever considered to be a part of these special teams. Looking back on these moments today it is easy for me to laugh and shake my head. How could I possibly have thought any of these ridiculous things after such a simple mission? At that moment however, these thoughts were breathtakingly real and rather than fight, I envisioned my own demise and shrunk down low in my seat on the ride back to camp, waiting for the inevitable. All this time, unbeknownst to me, the soldiers had radioed back to camp and passed along my condition to my commander. Everyone knew that something was wrong with me. To my soldiers and peers, I was not the normally calm and easy going leader they had eaten breakfast with just days before. Now as we returned to our outpost my operations commander was waiting at the gates. He gestured for me to step out of the vehicle and in a low voice he asked me for my weapon. I was done. My career and my life as I knew it was over. I was 'locked-in'.

8

THE LONG TRIP HOME

SUMMER 2005 / MEDEVAC HOME

As the weapon left my hands at the forward operating base in Afghanistan my mind was still reeling out of control. I silently begged for someone to please tell me what had happened to me. My former sergeant, SFC V, described what he saw in a letter later written on my request.[1] SFC V wrote: "I was with CPT Harris at that time and she was acting confused, tired and did not know what was going on. Speaking with her she was concerned that someone was going to hurt her and that she was in trouble for some reason that I could not understand."

To remove me from the current situation and the curious eyes of my soldiers, my commander decided it was best to return to our headquarters in the rear. CPT P took me to the backseat of his vehicle, closed the door and got in the front passenger's seat as we headed back to our main base. I felt like a prisoner without my weapon although in reality that was far from the truth. Everyone was worried about me, this was not the soldier or leader they had known for the last five years. The entire drive for me was spent in fear. I couldn't think straight. I was afraid to talk. My mind was racing, trying to "connect the dots" of the past few days. I was trying to figure out how all of this could have happened. Where did I go wrong? How could I have let myself get this bad? How could I have failed my soldiers so miserably?

Looking back on it now, how could such an inconsequential event cause me to freeze? A simple mistaken

---

[1] To better understand my state of mind and to catalog for my doctors what has happened to me over the years, I've asked former soldier, bosses and peers to describe what they saw during these episodes

alert to my fellow soldiers of a possible attack each of us in the vehicle felt imminent; why did it make me break down? How did it make me suddenly lose all control of my thoughts and actions? After everything I had been through in my life, my swimming, stress of the Academy, successes and disappointments, and potential life threatening missions from past deployments which had never bothered me before...Why now? Everything that had ever happened in my life was racing through my mind as I tried to figure out the situation I now found myself in. I was 'locked-in'. Due to the nature of the intelligence work I was doing before this mission, I now found myself trying to connect events, past missions, networks of friends and family to the current situation. My mind rapidly ran thru scenarios and memories of my past: my visits to the embassies to socialize with others, the children that I had helped build schools for, the missions we had performed in Iraq, or the warlord soldier that I had kicked out of our vehicle on our way to Bagram (all from previous deployments). Now I thought perhaps the enemy had found out where I was located and because of my previous encounters I was paranoid and believed "they" were determined to kill me and anyone that I was with. My unit no longer would want me because I was a threat to their security. I could share these conclusions with no one. How could I explain the events of my entire life, my whole thought process, to anyone in an hour long therapy session let alone my commander who now stood before me, examining strange reports from my soldiers about my behavior over the last 18 hours. He was trying to make a decision for my safety and that of my soldiers in less than five minutes.

During the ride back to basecamp, my commander and his driver tried to ease the tension and told jokes back and forth. But with the roar of the engine and my current state of mind, I couldn't really hear what they were saying. I believed they were joking and laughing about me. My mind was 'locked-in'.

When we arrived back at basecamp I was taken to my quarters, allowed to take a shower and call home. My peers were assigned to watch me 24/7. I wanted to talk to my parents but I also falsely believed that they would be ashamed of me. Stories they told and the pride they shared with friends about their daughter who was serving and protecting our country they would now have to explain to everyone that I had to be brought off the battlefield because I was weak and couldn't handle the pressure. I couldn't handle war. The only person I wanted to call was my grandmother. The only person I knew who would eagerly sit by my side and listen to all of my stories and woes of life, who cherished our short visits, who never criticized or judged me, only loved me. She was 89 at the time. She was a great mentor of mine, friend, and eventual roommate during graduate school. I wanted to hear a voice from home. I wanted to hear her voice. The satellite connection made her voice sound very distant and it was very hard to have a fluid conversation. Delays between what we each said were often times up to 30 seconds long. All I could say to her was that I was all right and how was her day going. How could I begin to tell her about my last 24 hours. How I had failed my soldiers and now I was a criminal, under arrest by my unit. My mind continued to wander again into crazy conclusions about my current situation. My fellow LTs watching me would switch out each hour. They cautiously tried to joke with me and let me know they were there for me. As each one finished their shift with me a new one would come in with curiosity as to why I was now a different person. Each one would bring another round of questions and concern. I couldn't answer a single question. I would mumble and just stare at them blankly, half the time in tears, half the time wondering what they were really thinking about me.

After another 12 hours of the same symptoms and again no sleep (going on 36 hours now) they decided to take me to the medical personnel on base. They quickly brought me over to the base hospital where I was laid on a gurney, IV placed, and surrounded by a team of medical personnel. Everyone believed I was in shock. I couldn't answer their questions. I just stared in horror, unable to comprehend that everyone around me was worried and trying to help me. A part of my mind was trying to tell me to snap out of it. There was nothing wrong with me, no one had gotten hurt. I had done nothing wrong. I was constantly battling inwardly wondering if I really was sick and in need of medical care, or if this was some test by the evaluators to see if I could handle the combat expected of a woman soldier applying to the SF special missions team. But if that sergeant back on my first deployment was right, if I couldn't disclose to anyone that I was being evaluated for this special forces team, I couldn't tell anyone because they didn't even know it existed. I eventually went numb. I tried to answer simple questions like my name, my unit and my SSN. I never fought them or had to be placed in restraints. I laid there in silence and complete and utter fear.

I was placed on the first combat MEDEVAC plane out of country. My Battalion commander, LTC P met me on the tarmac as my stretcher was carried onto the plane. I could see the look of concern in his eyes as he held my hand, but in my mind I knew he was glad I was no longer his responsibility. On the plane I was placed on a rack of stretchers that carried soldiers in critical condition home for additional surgery and care. There were soldiers covered in blood and screaming out in pain from gunshot wounds and missing limbs. I was assigned a very nice flight nurse who would occasionally hold my hand and tell me everything was going to be all right and then would sit a couple feet away and watch me the entire trip. A psych doctor also checked on me throughout the flight. He accompanied me everywhere and he was now the liaison to my current state of mind, ready to pass me off to the new doctors that would take on my case once we got to Germany. The guilt was starting to set in. Why would the Army waste its precious medical resources on me? Everyone must believe I'm faking all of this just to get out of the country and go home. I couldn't take the real taste of combat. I hadn't even been shot and here I was surrounded by soldiers that needed critical medical attention and I had taken one of the precious stretchers needed to carry them to safety. As we landed in Germany, I insisted on walking off the plane. I was not going to be carried off the plane on a stretcher when I obviously was not injured.

Once I arrived in Landstuhl, Germany I was taken into the American hospital and led to a locked unit; my first taste of a Psych ward. The doors slammed behind me and suddenly the full breadth of what had just happened over the last 48 hours was starting to set in. I was the only soldier in the ward that had just returned from the combat zone. I was dressed in combat fatigues and my boots were still covered in dust. The rest of the soldiers were local American soldiers stationed in Germany. Most were there due to suicide attempts, drug abuse, or threats to their commanders or other soldiers. I was the only woman on the unit at that time. There was no military rank or name tags used on the unit to distinguish between an officer or an enlisted soldier. We all wore hospital scrubs and my long hair had long lost what few precious hair ties I had with me, and the ward didn't carry anything but rubber bands. My laces from my combat boots that I still wore on my feet and the belt for my pants were stripped, removed, and put away for the threat that they posed to others. My pockets were emptied and my wallet and all my belongings were packed away in safes and bags so that they would not be used or stolen by others on the ward. I received daily advances from the patients on the wards. Many came and tried to tell me their sorrows and then pronounce their love to me. I just sat there in total silence. Afraid to talk, afraid of what others thought of me.

At one point I told a doctor that my breasts were secreting milk (I later learned that this was a side-effect of one of the medications). The doctor wondered out loud if I was pregnant, using this as an attempt to avoid the war. A wonderful nurse in charge of my care angrily cursed the doctor under her breath for his callous thoughts and ordered blood draws to prove to him I wasn't pregnant and of course, it all came back negative. I continued to have self-doubt as to why I was in the psych ward. Obviously, I was not cut out for officer material, I could not do my job. The Army no longer wanted me. I was making it all up. Five years of excellent ratings from my superior officers, five years of taking care of America's finest, beloved by my soldiers, respected by leaders, peers, and sergeants; everything had been thrown out the window. I had failed. All of the intense scrutiny of my story by the doctors in charge of my case wreaked havoc on my mental stability and confidence.

I spent my days in Germany attending mandatory group activities including childhood games like red rover, answering the endless questions of doctors in charge of my case, wandering the halls of the ward, and trying in vain to find peace and quiet so my mind could rest. When the patients and staff were given their 15 minute smoke breaks outside on the rooftop deck I jumped at the chance to be outdoors and breathe fresh air. But even these breaks were a stark reminder of my situation. As I breathed in the smoke filled air under gloomy overcast skies, I stared at the heavily draped concertina wire surrounding the borders of the roof meant to deter suicide attempts. I felt like a prisoner. A prisoner of the military and a prisoner of my mind, locked-in forever. As perplexed as my providers and myself were over my symptoms and my current state of mind, no one was prepared for what happened next.

As quickly as my mind fell into this scared paranoid state, I suddenly, after five days in the ward and eight days out of the valley, "snapped out" of my 'locked-in' state. I awoke to a new day. It was as if all the events of the last week were just a dream. I now stood before my doctors and the other patients on the ward with full confidence. I was back to my old self. I could carry on a regular conversation. I could explain in every detail what had happened to me over the previous days without loss of memory or recollection. I was ready to return to the desert, to my unit, to my soldiers in the field. As ready as I was to return, everyone else was skeptical. I would soon find out that this was only the beginning of my medical journey. The doctors wanted and needed further confirmation that I was sane. I was shipped off to the main Army Medical Center in Washington DC after two weeks.

BACK ON AMERICAN SOIL

JUNE 2005 / WASHINGTON DC PSYCH WARD

By the time I arrived at the stateside medical hospital in late June of 2005 I was at peace but embarrassed by what had happened. I had my confidence back. I marveled and laughed at my thought process over the past few weeks and I was ready to return to my unit in the field. The doctors, however, were not yet ready to give the OK. A person does not all of the sudden get better in a little over a week after basically losing all control in the midst of combat. That would require, according to them, intense counseling, medication, and weeks, maybe years, of therapy, to achieve reassurance that I was sane. Again, I was placed in the psych ward directly from the MEDEVAC flight with local soldiers from DC that were suicidal or threatening other soldiers and commanders in their units. Others had done drugs or were running away from UCMJ offenses or other legal problems. Some of these soldiers even confided in me during their stay on the ward that they were using the claim of mental instability to stay out of trouble. Again, I had to wave off advances from soldiers that were all male, mostly young privates and specialists that now had a woman in close quarters and confines of the ward. I was one of perhaps two officers on the unit. The other officer was refusing to go to war. I was put in front of medical panels, students, experts in all fields, and review boards. I underwent MRIs, CTs, daily lab draws looking for brain tumors and metabolic diseases. Strangely enough, I hoped something like this would be found that would explain what had taken over my mind. Anything to dismiss it was just my mind, soft, mostly subjective medicine that led me to decline so far and so fast without rhyme or reason. Each doctor and panel I met with had a different diagnosis and wanted to try a different medication: Bipolar, Brief reactive psychosis, PTSD, schizophrenia, anxiety, depression, illegal drug use, suicide, or just plain running away from my problems and life, faking my symptoms, or malingering. Doctors I met with were fairly certain that the war was not the cause of my problems. They believed this episode was something I was born with or the result of my childhood, or this mental break was going to happen regardless of my wartime experiences (perhaps this is true). I would always entertain the same questions with the same answers on a daily basis. No, I did not want to harm myself or others. Yes, I had come from a very loving family and had never been the subject of emotional or sexual abuse. No, my relationship with my father did not include sex as a young child. No, I did not hear voices in my head and I didn't see invisible people in the room around me. No, I did not feel my emotions included extreme highs and extreme lows that fluctuated throughout the year. Up until my episode I was an extremely confident, high functioning, happy young woman. I had been a good student in grade school and high school. I had always followed the rules growing up and no I did not hate my parents. I had never done drugs or had a problem with alcohol. I had never even smoked a cigarette. One doctor sat me down and lectured me about doing recreational and illegal drugs. He kept telling me I needed to come clean and get help for my drug problem. In his opinion this could be the only reason for my sudden 'locked-in' state, the inability to lead my soldiers. He theorized the drugs were out of my system by the time they had drawn my labs at the medical center. Opium was known to be readily available to soldiers from the locals who grew poppies in the fields that surrounded our base camps. Each denial by me was further evidence to him that I was lying. He reminded me there would be serious consequences even jail time for my drug abuse.

Returning to my thoughts about possibly being evaluated for the Special Operations female teams. I sometimes wrestled with the hope that at some point during all my travels through the psych wards someone would step out from behind a big curtain and say game over. Good job! Just kidding! All of this was a test and guess what, you failed miserably. I would wake up each morning hoping it had all just been a dream, and I would wake up back on my cot in the desert. I even pulled an emergency cord in the bathroom one day, hoping it would be my chance to say I'm throwing in the towel. I don't want to be tested like this anymore. I can't take it - just let me go home. But that never happened. The nurse reported this incident to my doctor, and he wrote notes about my obvious delusions-even a god complex - that caused me to pull the cord. I want to make it clear - during all these episodes, I never thought I saw people who weren't there nor was I unaware of where I was or my surroundings. If anything I sometimes hoped the cameras in the halls were really there to allow the 'man behind the curtain', the special operations team testing me, to secretly watch my actions. And most importantly, I do realize now that it was not a test - I really did have a mental break. No, I never could really explain this thought process to my doctors, and if I did it clearly sounded insane, therefore several of my early medical records and notes from the doctors describe my 'delusional' thoughts of grandeur of being considered for a special forces team that obviously did not exist. I know this because every time I saw a doctor or stayed in a psych ward, I asked for my medical records when I was released and I have copies of all of these records. I wanted to keep every record possible to provide it to future doctors who might be able to recognize a diagnosis.

Luckily, during all this I had a good group of friends and a very supportive family who made daily calls and sent cards, and books to the hospital to help me pass the time. Many attempted to visit me in DC. Yet, due to the nature of security on the ward only immediate family could visit for up to 15 minutes once a week. One friend was able to use his rank and visit me on the ward. He was my former mentor, Mike, back at West Point. This wonderful man and his wife, Jan invited me to their home on a weekend leave later during my stay and he tried to reassure me about my condition, speaking to me about his own struggles from his Army experiences.

Since the doctors didn't seem to have the answers I reached out to my step-brother, Josh, who was in medical school. I called him and quickly told him what happened to me. I hoped he had some insight having grown up with me and knowing the type of person I really was before my time in the Army. I remember he told me my stories sounded like a Hollywood movie and he was so happy I made it home safely, but I needed to follow the advice of my doctors because they were there with me now. The doctors had all the access to my medical charts and they knew best as to my current state of mind as I stood in front of them.

I never felt defeated, just frustrated and hopeful that all this skepticism from the doctors would soon pass. I began to wonder if I just wasn't explaining my thoughts and the events surrounding my demise well enough or in enough detail for the doctors to understand. I even had one doctor who stopped me in the middle of telling her a story after she had asked me what brought me to the ward. As I tried to explain the details and dangers of one of my missions, she cut me off and said she did not have a security clearance so she was not allowed to hear my accounts of what happened. I was at a loss with my providers. The doctors met with my friends and family and called back to the combat zone and talked to my commanders to ensure I hadn't been in trouble or broken any rules set by the military or the reason for my "mental break" was just me trying to run away from my problems. This always made me second guess myself and my own confidence in my leadership skills. To my knowledge, I had never broken any laws and my commanders confirmed this with the doctors. In my weak mental state I questioned why I declined so fast. I must have broken some unknown rule, or had some horrible unknown disease, or possibly had even been drugged and why couldn't the doctors figure out what was causing all of these things happening to my mind? Was I really the only person who exhibited these symptoms? My commanders back in Afghanistan and my family from home always assured the doctors I had been one of their best leaders in the unit and a good friend and daughter. My parents told the doctors I was a good, stable, happy kid growing up despite their divorce. They never worried about me and I never had a history of mental illness or a history of it in my family. I survived the tough criticism from the upperclassmen and the rigors of West Point. I also was able to easily juggle my time between a very good swimming career and academics, at least in high school. The doctors continued to come up empty in their attempts to find a mental health history that could explain my quick demise.

I remember towards the end of my stay at the medical center in DC, while I was waiting for a MEDEVAC flight out to my home base (this sometimes could take weeks), I was deemed "stable" enough to be allowed to take leave home to visit my family. Yet, when the doctor's found out I was to fly on a civilian aircraft and not drive the 8 hour trip home, they were overly concerned I would want to take over the controls and crash the plane. Because that's what they told me some mentally disturbed people are capable of when left alone. How could they believe that I would be capable of performing such atrocious acts? I was shocked and mortified. Waiting for the doctors to send me back to my home base would take weeks.

CAROLYN FURDEK

10

PASSING TIME

JUNE 2005 / WASHINGTON DC PSYCH WARD

Passing the time on the psych ward, sometimes the doctors would give us a chance to roam the confines of the hospital with a specialist or private in charge of us at all times. First we had to memorize the rules of leave from the ward and stand up in front of all the soldiers in group therapy each morning and spout off the orders. Once approved we were allowed to leave the locked doors and gain a sense of freedom. However nice this seemed, I felt the other patients and I could never seamlessly blend in amongst others. In my mind, we were always under the watchful eye of the other patients and doctors in the hospital easily recognized as mental cases without a missing limb and only seen as a danger to others. Sometimes I actually wanted to have lost a leg or been shot. In my condition, no one knew or could see the struggles of my mind. Much later I was reminded by a double amputee how lucky I was to receive the constant attention of the psychiatric community when I returned. He said he quickly dismissed the mental health doctors at his bedside during his recovery from the loss of his legs. Instead, he turned his attention and focus to his desire to walk again. Now, years later, he quietly suffers from invisible wounds that haunt him today.

Patients at the medical center in DC have daily visits from congressmen, senators, their commanders, hometown mayors, and even the President of the United States at their bedside to present them with awards for valor, purple hearts for their physical injuries, or just simply thank them for their service and their sacrifice for their country. These politicians, famous actors, popular businessmen and sports players frequented the halls of the hospital and amputee ward, writing blank checks for new houses and equipment. Quietly, outside media spotlights, they offered jobs and transportation for critically wounded soldiers and their families who were faced with almost insurmountable obstacles and costs to reintegrate back into society. But these special visitors were never allowed on the psych ward, even if they had ever wanted to visit. There were apparent privacy concerns, and we were considered too unstable and a possible security risk for their overall safety. Some patients probably should be considered a risk to others, but that was not true for all of us.

I once met a sweet lady, 'Regina', in a hospital elevator who was bringing homemade brownies to patients on a medical ward. She also had gifts from other people in the community, blankets and quilts made by little old ladies, and brand new electronics that had been donated to the wounded. When asked why I was a patient in the hospital, I sheepishly explained I was from the psych ward but I wanted her to know there were dozens of soldiers without visitors in my unit. 'Regina' immediately had sympathy. Here was someone who was not afraid of me or the ward. She wanted to bring the brownies and gifts to us. I led her to the doors, but we were quickly stopped and she was turned away by the staff. Soldiers on the other side could not have these 'luxuries' because we might hurt someone with them. The doors closed and locked behind me and 'Regina' walked away. I couldn't understand how homemade brownies or little old ladies' handmade quilts could ever be considered safety risks.

Assuming the role of a leader on the unit, I fell back into the need to take care of my soldiers. I never wanted sympathy for my situation, but I always wanted to help other soldiers in the psych ward, especially those who were depressed. The ones who no longer wanted to live. The desire to help these young struggling soldiers was especially important to me after I was in my right state of mind, but the doctors had either not observed me long enough or were too uncomfortable to label me as stable to discharge from the ward. For the suicidal patients, I advocated for them daily to the staff and doctors on the wards. I wanted staff to appreciate the need for additional resources and outlets for patients.

Finally, after constant requests, the soldiers and I were allowed to work out off the ward in the therapy pool or the stairwells (running flights of steps) and around the perimeter of the hospital with a staff member always close by. Staff also agreed to more volleyball time in the courtyard instead of just using the space for smoke-breaks.

You even had to ask permission to make a five minute public phone call home on one shared telephone, standing in a busy loud hallway with other patients waiting impatiently next to you to use the phone as well. Patients were unable to call anywhere except locally without a phone card. Often times I would use my personal telephone cards to allow the soldiers to call home and give away cards given to us in the warzone that the staff would not provide to stateside soldiers back home. Furthermore, computer and Internet access on the ward was not allowed, therefore soldiers, when given permission, would travel to a one desk office on a shared computer at a USO office outside of the ward, while patients on the other wards used free gifted computers at their bedsides. Our money, phones, and wallets were kept at the hospital bank and we had to wait in line to be issued our own money to even just visit the gift shop to buy a soda. Dealing with the restrictions and new rules, I longed for my freedom, yearned for time with my family, and tried to wait patiently to return to a normal life.

11

HOME

July - September 2005 / WEST COAST

I finally flew to my home base on another MEDEVAC flight in July of 2005, my standard mode of transportation and care the Army provided each time now as I returned to my final destination. I was handed over to another set of doctors in another psych ward because this was the "medical care" they believed would help cure me and keep me safe at the time. I was determined to show everyone I was normal and ready to return to my unit in Afghanistan. I did not want to leave the Army with a medical retirement because I apparently couldn't handle the pressure mentally. In my mind I could fight this. I was not sick. I was definitely not disabled. When I checked out of the psych ward a few days later, I had long been back to my old self and had proven myself stable by each set of doctors at each psych ward for the last 2 months. I was turned over to the care of my West Point classmate Marie's father, a retired General, who was my landlord and neighbor before I left the country. Prior to this last deployment, I lived in a beautiful house that sat on the water in a town outside of my post with Marie's parents as my neighbor's. I would awake to the smell of fresh bread on my door in the mornings and the couple would always join the young Lieutenants as we threw regular weekend parties. As he checked we out of the ward in 2005, he hugged me tight and welcomed me into his home. He and his wife served steak and fresh fish each night, and the general tried to comfort me with his stories of combat, and the struggles he still faced from the horrors of the Korean war over half a century ago. I was still ashamed and embarrassed about my reasons for having to leave my soldiers in the warzone. GEN R tried to remind me how hard it is for any soldier seeing the horrors of war, to forget and easily transition back into society.

Back at home, I took over a Brigade staff position and worked half days per my superiors' orders. I spent the days pushing paper and checking in on my soldiers still deployed. I longed to rejoin them. I passed my time reading books, attending mandatory therapy and counseling, and working out. While I was gone, my unit lost two more soldiers to an IED blast. One a fellow officer and the other was one of my favorite soldiers in the company. He had been with me as long as I had been in the unit. I immediately felt a sense of guilt for not being there to protect them with information I should have found, hopefully preventing the deadly attacks. It was difficult to ignore these feelings, and I constantly had to remind myself I was not in charge of my soldiers deployed or efforts of the enemy. Four months after my flight out of Afghanistan, my doctors at my post declared me sane. They discharged all my medications and stamped my paperwork for return to full unrestricted duty. They agreed with me that it must have been a fluke, something I ate, a momentary lapse of judgement, an electrolyte imbalance? Nothing in my medical review charts, nor the counseling I had gone through over the last four months, seemed to accurately describe the young energetic officer that now stood before them. I was fit for duty.

While the doctors had given their approval, my command was not as ready to return me to the fight. My Brigade commander, COL R, and a few staff officers I worked with were very concerned and reserved about my return to combat. However, one peer, CPT M, recently reached out and told me, while concerned, she also quietly cheered me on because she knew my personality. She also knew I normally functioned as a competitive, competent Army officer prior to and after this episode. She told me it was no simple task for anyone...only a true servant leader would have the desire to return to her soldiers in the field. My Brigade commander warned me he had read about soldiers pulled out before and then try to return to combat, only to quickly be brought out again with the same symptoms. COL R told me the Army would take care of me and I could quietly retire, move back to my hometown and start a family. He had the ability to do this for me and he wanted me to seriously take this offer into consideration. At this time, I had something to prove. I did not want to leave the Army with this on my record. Ultimately, he granted my persistent request to return to Afghanistan, but with much trepidation and concern. In September 2005 I was allowed to hop on a flight and rejoin my unit in combat. But this time I would take a job as an assistant officer in the Battalion supply room and stay far away from the intelligence arena and missions outside of the basecamp.

12

ONE MORE CHANCE

SEPTEMBER – DECEMBER 2005 / AFGHANISTAN

Upon my return to the desert, many in my unit familiar with how I had left just months before, walked on eggshells around me. The doctor who had flown on my flight out of Afghanistan and turned me over to the doctors at Landstuhl was shocked when he saw me in the chow hall after my return. Why had the Army let this obviously mentally broken soldier return to a combat zone let alone so soon? My commanders, after I left the first time, tried to keep the reports of my mental break at the construction camp from spreading needlessly. To the leadership team, the rest of the unit didn't need to know my condition. Besides, soldiers at the construction camp rarely returned to headquarters during the deployment; only those closest to me, my peers and other commanders knew of my condition at the time. However, rumors run rampant in the Army's small quarters. Though most soldiers in the unit found out and were leery about my return; they quickly learned I was my old self again and any doubts of my capabilities were erased. Nothing seemed out of the ordinary about my behavior. To them I was cheerful, helpful, eager, and wanting to share as much as I could with anyone willing to listen.

I was excited and confident of my abilities to handle a combat zone and a leadership role again. I wanted nothing more than to forget about the past events and return to the way things were before I left. I longed for my days in the Intelligence shop-for the respect I earned from my peers and my soldiers because of my knowledge and experiences in combat zones and the connections I had made with the other units on the base. Now I was the new rookie soldier in a combat zone. My soldiers had been in country going on seven months. I wanted to rejoin my unit and team in the operations center and get back in the fight. My past knowledge could "connect the dots" of the Taliban terror networks and the relationships and patterns of the attacks that happened to the soldiers outside the wire. But I knew better and stayed back in the supply room, ordering and pushing out supplies to our troops performing vital construction missions across the country. Other than the occasional mortar strikes aimed at our airbase or perimeter by the enemy, everything with my life on the airbase and my job in the supply shop was less stressful and manageable. Or was it?

In December of 2005, 4 months after my return to war, paranoia suddenly again set in. The supply room became a place of fear for me, bringing me back to the valley on that fateful day in May. Everything COL R had warned me about, all the concerns from my family that were relayed to me before I deployed, all of the caution and trepidation COL R had given me back home before I left came to fruition. My former sergeant, SFC V, wrote a letter for me after the fact describing again what he saw: "In the beginning of December she became unsure of herself and was asking me questions to convince herself that everything was okay. She again became afraid that someone was after her and it was clear she could no longer function or take care of herself in theater." Suddenly, in my mind, I found myself back in the valley in the summer of 2005, memories flooding back. I lost all confidence in my abilities. My mind raced. Cecil, a fellow captain who took me to the infirmary at the time mentioned recently "It was really scary watching someone who'd been so sharp become completely lost in her own thoughts. It was like watching someone who was hypnotized still talking with you but clearly in a dream world." SFC V accompanied me on the MEDEVAC flight out of country and further wrote "During the trip she was unsure why she was going back and very concerned with her future. She was

unable to sleep during the flights even though she was medicated."
I was 'locked-in', again.

This time I was fast tracked back to America through the MEDEVAC system. My doctors had a paper trail of medical records from my previous episode to fall back on and guide them in their decisions and necessary medications that they thought would help me recover. As the doors shut on the psych wards in Germany, DC, and my home base, I knew the drill. I knew the forthcoming questions, the medical staff that would observe me with a skeptical eye, the strange rules meant to keep us safe and the loss of my shoelaces and belts for my "safety" and the safety of other soldiers in the ward. As I returned to the ward, it was as if I had never left. The staff knew me and I knew the rules. The patients again harassed me and the staff again seemed unaware of their advances. With the stark walls, dilapidated conditions and annoying patients, I quietly tried to find my peace and recover.

And just like that, just like before, for no rhyme or reason and to everyone's surprise, I quickly returned to reality and my worries and paranoia were gone. I suddenly, like a light switch, snapped out of my 'locked-in' state. The physicians tossed around diagnoses of schizophrenia, never wanting to believe my symptoms could result from my time in combat. Everyone knew it was the end of my time in the Army. After the quick recovery of my symptoms in Landstuhl, I was ready to fly home and get out of the Army. Yet, I had to go through the system again, spend two weeks at each psych ward under doctor's scrutiny and wait for MEDEVAC flights to each new destination.

I spent my mandatory observation weeks in the wards and eventually in the barracks on the medical bases trying to make the best of my situation. I took on the role of a leader and advocate for my fellow patients and soldiers on the ward. I tried to help the soldiers who were depressed and suicidal find hope. I found and pressed the staff for additional unorthodox activities to fill our time. I secured more physical training opportunities in stairwells and therapy pools for patients under staff supervision, believing strongly that natural endorphins were easily obtained from a vigorous workout. Soldiers are expected to keep themselves in top shape every day in the armed forces to meet the demands of combat. Here on the ward, exercise was not a priority and did not happen very often. Smoke breaks and TV time were seen as more appropriate uses of our time when therapy and counseling sessions with doctors were not in session. Endless days of coloring with crayons and completing the same 1000 piece puzzles with the same missing pieces dragged on. Furthermore, our bedroom doors were locked closed before breakfast to prevent any patient from trying to be alone or sleep all day. Instead we were relegated to the common area with 20 other patients and shared one TV and a box of crayons. Even after spending 20 hours a day surrounded by dozens of soldiers in combat, my requests for solitude, quiet time and rest were dismissed.

I finally returned back to my home base; back to my Brigade staff job in January of 2006. The Army declared me 50% disabled. I would retire with full military benefits including health care for life. I was grateful for the Army's care but embarrassed for the reasons I was leaving the service. It still took months to finish all my paperwork and medical files to transition out of the Army. I watched my soldiers return from Afghanistan in April of 2006. They returned with less soldiers than when they deployed over a year prior. These soldiers were lost to IEDs, suicide and the enemy. Again, I pushed back the feelings that I had failed them because I had not been able to control my mind. I had accepted my fate. I had to leave the Army on disability. I would find a new career where I would not be responsible for the lives of others. I was ready to move on as they stamped my final paperwork in May of 2006. With hopes of a career in the FBI now dashed, I still felt I could handle a high level stressful job. I still felt I had something to prove. I was not disabled. My mind was not broken. Little did I know, this was not the end of my struggle and my medical mystery.

13

LIFE AS A CIVILIAN

Before I signed my final leave paperwork in the Army in 2006, I got a job offer in Washington D.C. Not surprisingly, it was along the same lines of intelligence/engineer work I performed in the Army for the previous six years, but this time deployments were not required. I believed I could handle this kind of work and so did my new boss. My work would still require a security clearance. With my mental history I did not think I would be allowed to have such a clearance but surprisingly, in the civilian world, this was accepted as what sometimes happens to people in very stressful situations. I gave full disclosure of my past mental health history in the security clearance process and informed one of my new bosses of my medical history before I was hired. They still offered me the job and the pay was amazing. I traded my camouflage and combat boots for a skirt and a pair of heels and I moved to the nation's capital. I quickly made myself at home in the new company and new town. The daily routine was not very demanding and I felt like I was contributing to a greater good. During this time in Washington DC I used my Army retirement funds to pay for civilian doctors to provide additional therapy outside of the VA and peruse my mental health history, always seeking new medical opinions. Yet, the civilian doctors continued to be just as baffled with my symptoms and could not give me a diagnosis or recommend a medication different than the ones prescribed by the military and the VA.

After sitting in front of a computer at a desk for four months, I started to get a little bored and I longed to be out in the community working face to face with people again. I still yearned for new challenges and adventure. With my clearance and my job I could never return home and talk about work with family or friends. One of my bosses MM, would always tell her friends that she was in charge of planning and providing the music being played in elevators throughout DC and she was good at it.

With Friday's off, I looked to the volunteer department at the Army medical center in the city. It was fun to again meet and thank the little old lady who had met me off the MEDEVAC flight and return the hug she had given me when I first arrived at the hospital. Now, one year later, I was given the opportunity to volunteer in the Physical Therapy department. I had gone through Physical Therapy four times for my knee in my youth. When I was eleven years old I tore my ACL during a bicycle accident (I was actually racing a boy at the time). I was told at the time I was the youngest ACL repair operation that had ever been performed in the United States. After surgery in 1990, I had months of PT and admired the education and dedication of the therapists who worked with me. I tore it again quickly after my first operation but since it was relatively stable and I didn't play a contact sport, we all decided it was best to wait until I stopped growing when a more permanent surgery could be performed. Prior to joining the Army at the age of 17, I went through this operation in order to gain admittance to the Academy. I eventually required two additional surgeries due to my constant desire to push my body to its limits. These surgeries were both performed at West Point. Each time I had to endure months of post-operative rehabilitation. It was not fun answering my doctor's questions about why he had seen me running on post, three weeks after my third surgery, when I was still supposed to be on crutches. This is likely the reason I had to undergo four surgeries to finally fix my knee.

There was a reason I was allowed to quickly integrate into the volunteer office and work in the physical therapy department. Back in 2005, while I was a patient on the psych ward at the Army hospital in DC, waiting to return home to my post, I found out the physical therapy department had a therapy pool in the hospital for amputees and other soldiers recovering from battle injuries. I begged my psychiatrists to let me swim, assuring the doctors it would be very therapeutic for me and a welcome change. At the same time I learned there was a pool, I also learned my physical therapist from West Point, LTC S. was the commander of the Physical Therapy Department at the army medical center where I was a patient. When she found out what happened to me, knowing my swimming skills from my time at the Academy, she pulled some strings with my doctors and got me lap time in the therapy pool. Despite the 96 degree water temperature, I loved the feel of the water and the freedom and solitude it provided away from the ward.

Now, in the fall of 2006, LTC S was still the commander of the department and after discovering my interest in PT, she quickly asked for me by name in the volunteer office and integrated me into her staff and her department. Some of my doctors who were following me at the time were worried working with trauma victims would trigger new episodes but it never did or has to this day. I quickly learned my new role and loved working with patients and helping them walk again and learn new skills to adapt to their injuries.

With a full-time job, good friends, regular visits from family and satisfying volunteer work, my life appeared to be back on track. My doctors followed me closely during this time and monitored my activities and stress. We all hoped this change in lifestyle would afford me a normal life again. Yet, as we all quickly learned, my mind would never settle. The memories and stress of my past deployments, quietly simmered, waiting for the opportunity to escape and upend my life once again.

14

A REVOLVING DOOR

November 2006 / WASHINGTON DC

In November/December 2006 my calm, non-stressful civilian life came crashing down again. This time, I was six months out of the Army and living with my roommate, Melody, in Washington DC. I visited some old high school friends at a college swim meet the night before and for some reason the unfamiliar surroundings and change in my daily routine built up additional stress and my paranoia and fear took over once again. It started with the loss of my confidence in the presence of my friends. I panicked and quietly became suspicious of those around me, afraid to talk to them and afraid to even join them for dinner. This time I was no longer in a combat zone. I no longer had rockets flying above my head, but all the memories of previous deployments came flooding back. I was in the valley again, I had failed my soldiers. Now I had failed my current boss. I couldn't even make it in the civilian world doing a desk job. The next morning I sat frozen at my desk, and having not slept the night before, I could not answer my boss's concerned questions. I couldn't perform a simple task. I looked at her helplessly and fearfully. She asked me if I was on some recreational drugs and told me it was okay - I could tell her.

My boss was somewhat aware of my mental health history. In a letter written to my providers at my request she reported: "Carolyn's behavior at work was abnormal. She was in a very confused state and seemed to be unable to engage in normal work activities or conversations. I considered her to be in a nonfunctional state. If I had been unaware of previous medical issues, I would have thought she was under the influence of drugs or alcohol. However, I was certain that this was not the case of Carolyn." Knowing I was not acting right, she took me to a psychologist that was a friend of her family. My boss planned on taking me home with her after the session for the weekend, but the doctor was concerned with my current state of mind and asked her to take me to the local civilian hospital and ER. MM called my mother who sent her good friend from nursing school to my bedside until she could make arrangements and travel to be by my side. While we waited for the doctors my step-sister, Marney, got on the phone with me and would not let me hang up for five hours trying to keep me calm. After my mental condition continued to worsen, I agreed to go to the psych ward. Hours later I found myself surrounded again by people who were suicidal, mad at the world or talking to imaginary people. My mind raced with memories of the desert. Attempting to battle my own mind, I constantly questioned myself: How could I let this happen again? What was the trigger? Why couldn't I control my life? Why was I so weak? As I sat crying in my hospital room, I asked the doctor what was going on. He tried to convince me that I was the sickest one on the ward and they wanted to help me.

Within a few hours, my father and mother were by my side. In this psych ward they were allowed to stay with me as long as I liked. After a day of watching me sulk in my bed, my mom lovingly dragged me out of my room, put me under a cold shower and brushed my hair. Moments later I was back to my old self (I wish this method had cured me every time). After just 36 hours of hospitalization I was released to the care of my mother. Instead of firing me (as I had prepared myself for), my boss gave me some medical leave and wanted me to return to the company with an adjusted plan that would not require intelligence type work. I spent the next few weeks celebrating the holidays with my family and planning my next move. Everyone, including me, decided I needed to get out of the intelligence business, leave DC and find a new career (unfortunately, until I could save up the money to pursue an advanced degree, this would not happen for another year). We all assumed intelligence work was my trigger.

At the time, I was enjoying the volunteer work I was doing at the Army Hospital every Friday. I began to wonder if a career in the medical field, specifically physical therapy might provide less stress in my career and provide my mind a chance to truly heal.

One particular patient I had the privilege of meeting in the therapy department made my decision to switch careers easy. His story was both tragic yet inspiring. He was a medic by trade, always running to the injured on the battlefield. This time he was on the other end, riding in a vehicle hit by an IED. Just about every bone in his body was broken by the impact and he had been through dozens of surgeries by the time I saw him, spending almost a year at the Army Medical Center in DC as the doctors put him back together. He showed up to the physical therapy clinic in his wheelchair every day with a smile on his face, ready to endure the pain of recovery, ready to push himself farther physically with each painful exercise and activity. One day I asked him how he did it. How could he always be so happy. He told me, "There were four other soldiers in my vehicle that will never come home. I got to live another day and return to my friends and family." He explained "What reason do I ever have to complain?" After he told me this, I thought I too had no reason to ever complain. I was determined to make the most of every day and what better way to fulfill that desire than to help others, newly injured or recovering from disease, to make the most of their day as well? Thinking of this soldier and the interaction the physical therapists had with patients like him each day, motivated me to drop everything I knew. I decided to leave my comfort zone, and step out into the unknown.

15

ANOTHER DOOR OPENS

2007 / WASHINGTON DC

When I returned to DC from the holidays with my family in January of 2007, I had already applied and been accepted at a local community college to take online classes in anatomy and biology, prerequisites required for physical therapy school. My mind was made up. I would go to graduate school and become a physical therapist, now requiring the completion of a doctoral degree program. I was not going to be considered broken and disabled and let my mind and it's memories crush my life endeavors. My doctors were very concerned that I was going to pursue such an advanced degree. They tried to warn me patients with my wounds often could not handle the stress and academics from such a rigorous program and they didn't think I had the mental fortitude to finish the degree. This time I ignored their concerns, their views on my intelligence, and set my sights on a career in health care.

As I pushed through the next year and a half of prerequisite courses, my nights and weekends were spent studying and riding my bike to a local community college to take tests in proctored computer rooms. My vacations were spent doing homework, research projects and writing papers. Most of my leisure time I enjoyed for the last 7 years since college was gone. Without the rigors and pressures of Academy life, I was able to easily pull off A's in all my classes and still continue working a full time job. I told my bosses very early on of my plans. While not completely understanding my willingness to leave a very good, high paying job, my boss loved and respected my new found passion and dedication. My departing gift from her was a keychain that still holds my car keys to this day. The key chain reads: Live the life you love, and love the life you live. I couldn't agree more!

I continued to volunteer at the Army Medical Center in DC, getting exposure to all the different areas of physical therapy practice at the hospital. I quickly learned what I had feared most as a patient on the psych ward. There are still many providers in health care that do not understand mental illness. One day I shadowed a PT around the hospital as he made his daily rounds. He quickly sped up and bypassed the psych ward where I was a patient myself just two years prior. He ignored a doctor's order for a PT evaluation/consult for a soldier on the ward. He explained to me he never went on the ward because the patients were crazy and he questioned if they even needed our help. It took me a while to want to return again to the hospital, frustrated and hurt by his thoughts of patients on the wards. After much encouragement from my family, I came back and confronted this therapist about his views of the soldiers behind those doors and tried to advocate for their care. I tried to explain that a soldier may need his help, and to not discount them so readily. When he scoffed at my suggestion and reasons I didn't give up and turned toward my old therapist, the commander of the department, to see if she felt the same as her employee. She assured me it was not the policy of the department and she would speak with this therapist to ensure he didn't ignore the orders again.

My full-time job, my college studies, and my volunteer work consumed all my time and kept my mind at bay and peaceful. I closed out the 2007 calendar year with a pretty uneventful winter. The only somewhat stressful event that year was breaking off a relationship that wasn't meant to be. I'm so grateful now for the people I crossed paths with in my life. That old boyfriend inspired me to go back to graduate school at an older age, since he himself was in law school well into his 30's. I was proving to myself, my doctors, and my family I could handle this stress called life, like I always had before that fateful day back in 2005. I survived an entire year without an episode.

I was prepared to pay for the tuition of the doctoral program required to attain a PT license by myself. I was certainly surprised when a former swim team friend, Jenn, told me I earned the benefit and qualified for assistance from the Veteran's vocational rehabilitation program. I initially scoffed, thinking that should only be reserved for high school educated soldiers who never had the opportunities to go to college, or seriously injured soldiers who could no longer do the job for which the Army trained them. My friend encouraged me to apply, reminding me I was a soldier and veteran too who was no longer able to perform the job I had done in the Army or in the civilian world. I could now possibly be a valuable asset in a new career field and the VA wanted to support me and see me succeed. I applied to the vocational program and the VA counselor happily accepted me. I had to test academically for the appropriateness of the career and I was told I surpassed all tests. The VA agreed being a Physical Therapist was a good fit for me and I could handle the academics. They were also going to pay for the tuition, give me a monthly stipend, and provide me with a computer and all course books to succeed. If I needed a tutor they could provide that as well. The program wanted to ensure I had every tool available to achieve my goals. They told me to find a school I wanted to attend, gain admission and they would take care of the rest. Against all advice and better judgement, I put all my eggs in one basket and applied to only one PT school with a well-respected program, Bellarmine University, in Louisville, Kentucky. My grandmother lived nearby. I loved her and her city. I knew I needed stability and family during school, but I didn't want to move close to my mother and father (I love them dearly but that felt too much like going back home). Besides my grandmother, I had several aunts, uncles, and cousins in town eager to help me pursue my new career and watch over my well-being.

I turned in my application to the University in October of 2007 and eagerly anticipated word of my acceptance. My grade point average at West Point was a 2.7. Never a good number to apply to graduate schools. I often heard the rigors and demands placed on cadets from the academies were considered when applying to some graduate schools. Rumor had it, grade point averages from the academies could be raised as much as an entire point by an accepting graduate program. I asked the director, Mark, (on an early visit to the program) if this was the case at his school. He quickly dismissed this hope but said they did look for non-traditional students who could bring a different background to the career field. Also, my hard work in the prerequisite courses had finally paid off and all the A's were now added in to my overall GPA from West Point. With this confidence, and following a promising interview with a professor, Beth, at the program, I packed up my bags, gave my leave notice to my boss (never to make that kind of money again), and drove west to Kentucky on January 1st, 2008. As luck would have it after driving over 10 long hours alone from DC, eager to see my grandmother and yearning to just finish my trip, I was pulled over by a cop for speeding one mile from my Grandmother's house. The officer, apparently not believing I was literally driving into town that day, reminded me I only had 30 days to get a KY driver's license and change my plates. He wondered out loud why I ignored the deadline after my arrival.

I quietly started my new life in Kentucky. My grandmother insisted I live with her as she lived alone in a four bedroom house and she wanted the company. I happily obliged. My grandmother has always been a positive part of my life. She grew up on a farm outside of the city, rode horses bareback, and climbed trees with the boys. She had attempted to attend medical school at the University in the 1930's, only to be denied entry because she was a woman. She later went on to marry my grandfather and raise three wonderful, caring children. With 10 grandchildren and 24 great-grandchildren, she marveled at the size of her family being she was an only child. My grandmother eventually lived past 100 and was well known in the children's hospitals as a volunteer at 95, as a regular visitor to the elderly in the nursing homes at 98 and still managed to get down on the floor at 100 years young to play with her great grandchildren. Her home for 66 years was meticulously organized and renovated by my grandfather with a finished attic and basement. It was a place of life and love for the entire family. Her gardens were always full of prize-winning roses she tended to till the last few weeks before she died, and she always had a fresh bouquet for family and visitors she never turned away. As her roommate, I got to hear a centuries worth of amazing stories and wisdom and I tried in vain to keep up with her busy social calendar.

Three months after my arrival to town, in the spring of 2008, I awaited my acceptance letter from the physical therapy program. I held a part time job as a PT technician at a local outpatient clinic, paying minimum wage, with a boss who always told me I was way overqualified for the position. My boss at the clinic knew I wanted to be a PT and appreciated the fact I wanted as much exposure as possible to my future career field. I answered telephones, washed towels, emptied trash cans and cleaned off tables. In return he would teach me techniques, exercises, anatomy and help me understand the different diagnoses therapists come across in the medical field and how we as Physical Therapists could help them. I finished up the last of my prerequisite classes for PT school at another local University in late April, 2008. I still had not received a letter of acceptance from Bellarmine. The new class of PTs was supposed to start in May. From the day I applied back in October, I sent weekly emails to Mark, the director of the PT program. The subject line always read: Engineer in DC. The topic mainly centered around my interest in the program, the qualities and background I could bring to the program and the profession, and my yearning desire to be a physical therapist and help others return from their injuries. Because I was a non-traditional older student in another state applying to a program that accepted most of their candidates from the undergraduate program at their school, I knew my odds of earning a seat in the class were slim. I wanted Mark to remember me. Occasionally, I would get a message back stating he was glad I applied and to keep putting forth the good effort. He always added if I was not accepted this year I could always apply the following year.

Finally, I got a phone call from the secretary at the University. They were waiting for my acceptance letter to attend.

The program used my old mailing address in DC from my application in October and my offer letter had been floating around somewhere on the east coast for the last 3 months. I was told I had one day to accept the offer and turn my deposit into the program. I drove over to the University as soon as possible and secured my seat. Finally, my life was going in the right direction. I could prove to everyone I was not broken. I was not disabled.

16

BACK TO SCHOOL

2008 / LOUISVILLE, KY

When school started in the Physical Therapy program at the end of May 2008, I was like a little kid again. I bought my school supplies weeks in advance, laid out my clothes for the first day of classes the weekend before, and jokingly had my grandmother take my picture as I left for my first day of school. Compared to the rest of my classmates, I was ten years their senior and one of the few that lived outside their parent's home. I started my first class with 47 other mostly young 21 year-old students, ready to tackle the next 2.5 years of a 4 year compressed doctoral program. Most of the students in the program were fresh out of college, some not even of age to drink, or were using the first year in PT school as their senior year of college. I was old to them, but they accepted me and invited me to their study groups and out to the bars in the evenings with what little freedom we allowed ourselves from the rigors of studying. Life with my grandmother as a roommate was better than expected. She was a great study partner and she loved to hear my stories from school and the new topics I was learning. I had a curfew of eight o-clock, which my future fiancé was even required to follow, and new house rules which I happily adjusted to, forcing me to dedicate more time to studying. I cherished my grandmother's company, her advice, her stories of the past, and her hope for the future. Throughout my entire life our visits together were never more than a week or two for holidays or summer vacations. Now we were roommates and she had the energy of a forty year old woman rather than a woman almost seven decades my senior. We would head out every Thursday and find a new restaurant to explore. I would help her with her roses and accompany her on her long walks outside, discussing life, listening to her wisdom or simply enjoying each other's company. My grandmother said she was grateful for the car at her disposal, as I willingly drove her around on her errands and the busy social schedule this 90+ year-old woman managed to a fault. Although I always offered, she mainly cooked our dinners, encouraging me to eat my vegetables again. It was nice to come home to a warm meal and someone in the house eager to hear about my day; a welcome change after 12 years away from my parents' home. My classmates all loved her and the PT program talked of making her an honorary graduate. They loved that she would come out and compete in our 5K runs around the zoo and participate as a mock patient in our study groups. She said she equally enjoyed having young life back in her house. She relished the chance to leave the confines of her home and explore the ever-changing landscape and roads she had grown up around all of her life. The first semester flew by and halfway through my 2nd semester I thought I had finally left the wounds and all my failures behind. After all, I had made it through all of 2007 and most of 2008 without an episode to stop me in my tracks.

It was the fall of 2008. Nothing very stressful or different was happening in my life. I successfully finished the first semester of PT school, completed another Ironman triathlon, and met a new guy I enjoyed spending time with and who would eventually become my spouse. Life by all accounts was normal. However, my mind had other plans for me. My mind was not ready to settle, my mind was still fragile and wounded.

I was sitting in a lecture with the professor talking about prescription drugs. The day of classes was like any other with the stress of tests looming every week. Yet for some reason as I contemplated my usual plans panic began to set in and suddenly I found myself back in the valley. I could feel the weight on my shoulders, the goosebumps I would get on my arms, the foreign thought processes start to creep into my mind and slowly I began to lose confidence in all my abilities. My table and study mate,

Jill, well aware of my health struggles I had confided in her after we became close friends, picked up on my uneasiness right away. She sat beside me and worryingly watched as I began to unravel before her. She later recalled, "[she was] mostly insecure and somewhat socially avoidant. As a few days went by the insecurity became paranoia, and the social avoidance became an inability to be in a heavily populated room without feeling uncomfortable and restless....she seemed to be doing more of a 'daydreaming-like activity....I truly believed that Carolyn might cause herself permanent damage to her brain if something was not professionally assessed and done." Jill hoping to quietly remove me from any further stress drove me straight home to my grandmother. I sat with my friend and my grandmother gradually getting worse and further 'locked-in'. Jill decided it was time to get some medical intervention and led me to her car. I pleaded with her at the car door. Begging her to keep me away from the doctors and the hospital. Jill new better and thought it best to get me professional help. She drove me and my grandmother to the local Veterans hospital. In the ER the first thing the doctors asked for, once they observed my behavior and my symptoms, was a urine and blood sample. Hoping to quickly diagnose a drug problem or addiction, they felt this was the root cause of my current presentation. As the tests came back negative, the doctors realized their first impression was wrong and they started to delve into my mental health records. I made my grandmother promise early on when I first moved in to never let them take me back into a psych ward, to avoid them at all costs. Now they were talking about doing just that and she was getting more and more frustrated with the doctors, trying desperately to keep her promise. I just sat there frozen and unable to comprehend that it could possibly be happening again. My aunt and uncle arrived to relieve my friend and grandmother, reluctantly letting the doctors convince me to voluntarily check myself into the psych ward at the hospital. My doctors explained to my family and me that I needed to be closely followed and monitored on a locked unit as new medications were prescribed to control my symptoms. To this day, I truly believe no medication except the one I now take was able to stop or prevent my symptoms, ever!

Nobody could understand why it was happening again. Clearly I was not coming from a combat zone and my life was not in any imminent danger. This time the doctors at the VA had sympathy for my condition, after dealing with so many Vietnam and World War II veterans who struggled with flashbacks and memories of wars they fought so long ago. But as I stood before them I was unable to function and everyone was worried about me. This time when the doors closed behind me on the ward, I lost all hope that I would ever be cured of these invisible wounds. Again, as the only woman on the ward, I had to fight off advances from older veterans, while at the same time feeling trapped in my mind and dealing with my own issues. At night I would hear my door rattle and then hear a nurse in the hall call out to the patient at my door to return to his own room. I would mention these incidents to the doctors in the morning, but I was hastily told I must be hallucinating or believe people were there who did not exist. With only one shower room, the showers were shut down to the rest of the patients while I took mine. Occasionally, a patient would try to slip past staff guarding the bathroom door and join me in the shower. Fortunately, staff were always able to stop him but not before he got the chance to see me without my clothes. I learned to take quick showers, never put my back to a door, and stay in my room away from the common areas as much as I was allowed. I hardly had an appetite and didn't feel the need to participate in the classes meant to deter one from suicide or breaking a drug addiction. In my mind, all the nurses and staff on the ward were skeptical as to why I was there. As if warding off the advances from fellow patients wasn't enough, I had a medical student assigned to my case that mentioned he wanted to lay down in my bed next to me during one of our daily therapy sessions. He also gave me his phone number and suggested I call once I was discharged from the hospital. I was also attracted to him at the time and appreciated the attention from someone other than a patient, but I understand now the dangerous doctor/patient relationship line he crossed and am grateful it did not go any further.

Just like the previous two episodes, my mind finally released its paralyzing grasp on my life. After one week in the ward, I was back to my old self and wanted to return to the PT program. Again, my doctors were perplexed. Anxious to move along and have my friends and family again, I yearned to leave the confines of the ward. I requested to join the other patients on a supervised outing on the other side of the locked doors. Stabilized patients were given the opportunity to leave the ward to go to the gym or snack shop in the hospital. The doctors were not as anxious as I to set me free. They still had concerns over my sanity and wanted to observe me for a longer period of time. In my case, I was told if I wanted to go outside the ward it meant I was ready to be discharged home but they were not ready to let me go. The nurses wondered why I had not packed a suitcase for my visit to the ward and instructed my family to bring clothes for me and shampoo in efforts to make me feel more comfortable as they continued to observe my actions and demeanor.

To better explain admissions to psych wards, most patients are admitted for a minimum two week observation period. The clock can easily be reset if the patient takes a step backwards or causes any concern for the doctors. Each patient's circumstances are different. For some of the long-term patients, who could sometimes spend months on the ward, they were allowed short supervised visits with the general population, mainly to go smoke and buy snacks. Reasons for their release and not mine still baffle me to this day.

One of my professors, Beth, visited regularly while I was on the ward and brought class notes and homework that I missed. I had my books and study material with me on the ward, locked in a room the staff controlled and occasionally they would allow me to pull them out. Counting the days of school I missed, I tried desperately to stay current with my classes. The staff on the ward would not allow me to take my binders back to my room for fear the metal in the rings could cause harm. I was only allowed to sit on the floor in the hall in front of the nurses station with my binders in clear view spread out in front of me. Studying in these conditions with patients constantly roaming around my papers and stepping on my books was never ideal or very productive.

Eager to find better use of my time, I fell back into the role of caregiver, advocate, and provider for the patients on the ward. I would see patients limping from old war injuries or complaining about common back injuries and muscle strains. I tried to advocate to get the PT's in the hospital to come and work with these patients on the ward. But my pleas seemed to fall on deaf ears. Often times if a physical therapist has an order to evaluate a patient on the ward who does exhibit a physically limiting injury, attempts to teach a patient with a psychiatric disorder new stretches and exercises for often old chronic physical injuries is very difficult. The patients hardly follow thru with exercises and their appointments to visit physical therapists outside the wards are often ignored.

Once I was finally discharged from the ward, I tried to jump back into my classes at school. Unfortunately, I missed too many days during my medical leave of absence. The program appropriately warned us from the beginning that due to the fast paced condensed program, even one missed day of class was very hard to make up and stay current with the studies. To make it fair for everyone, there was a limit on the number of classes we could miss. I had far surpassed the limit for the semester. I was told I could restart the semester over again with the new class the next fall and take a few of the 2nd year classes with my original classmates in the spring and summer to remain current. Thinking I wouldn't want to do this, the director, Mark, pulled me into his office, praised me on my work thus far, and wished me good luck on my future endeavors. When he learned I wanted to continue, he was surprised, but quickly came up with a program to keep my skills up with additional classes, including shadowing a great mentor of mine in school, Dennis. Dennis is a physical therapist who mainly works with amputees, and is considered a local expert for their needs and therapy program. With his guidance, I studied everything I could about the technology available to them and the role a therapist plays in helping an amputee walk again.[2] This break from the standard therapy program at Bellarmine was refreshing and very rewarding. According to Mark, I could repeat the fall semester with a new class of PT students in August of 2009. My life had taken another turn, something I was now getting used to in my life. Without school as my main focus, I had extra time on my hands to pursue new interests, socialize with friends, and spend some more time with a guy from our local running group. Little did I know that this brilliant, kind-hearted man would soon change my life forever.

---

[2] My capstone project for the culmination of my studies in the therapy program focused on amputees, and together we created a great tool, an education program to help other therapists understand how they could help patients missing limbs, and how to develop a recovery program

17

THERE WAS THIS GUY...

During the early spring of 2008, a wonderful man named Glenn, (who happened to be a distant relative) invited me out to some Tuesday night track workouts with a local running club. He boldly introduced me to a young engineer who he felt sure would be a good match. I was instantly attracted to this young man named Joe, but his running skills far exceeded mine and I never had the chance to keep up with him or get to know him better during the workouts. After attending several months of track workouts I was invited to join a local running group, the Dawn Chasers. This group provided me some new friends, outside of school and also closer to my age. I also had a chance to improve my running skills and hang out with Joe. Larry, the owner of a local running store, started the group in the late 80s maybe 90s as legend has it and it had grown over the years to include members of all ages and skill levels. Members can show up to a set location and time, and run the empty streets with fellow early risers, up to 10 miles as the sun rises over the Bluegrass. Afterwards, the runners head to a local coffee shop and socialize before the rest of the world awakes.

During the summer of 2008, Joe finally took notice and seemed to enjoy my abilities to surpass him in the pool and during triathlon races. My mother, who feared I may intimidate the boys, had always warned me to "let the guys win". This guy didn't seem to mind and the other members of the Dawn Chasers encouraged my interest and tried to push things along between the two of us.

Initially, having just moved to the area and found a great group of people who shared my running interest, I brushed off their suggestions for fear of awkwardness and embarrassment if things did not work between us. I figured since he had been in the group longer than I, I would be the first one asked to forgo my membership amongst my new friends. So we casually hung out with friends throughout the summer and fall. One of the runners in the group, Kevin, was very persistent and would constantly fall back to my running pace and remind me what a good man Joe was, telling me he would make a wonderful husband and father. Having finally given up my fears of dating him, I waited for Joe to make the first move all summer. Forever inpatient and wanting to get to know him better, I finally asked Joe out on our first date in the early fall of 2008. I quickly asked my classmate Jill from school to join us at the last minute so the pressure would not be overwhelming. To my surprise, we all enjoyed ourselves, including Joe.

Shortly after I was discharged from the hospital from the latest episode in 2008, I called Joe and left a message. This caring concerned man who had only gone on our first date, called me back within the hour to check on me. Apparently these episodes did not scare him away. I figured no guy would ever want to settle down with a "crazy" lady like me, with all this "baggage". I soon discovered Joe was very different than the loud, sometimes overly self-confident guys I normally hung around with in the Army and thought I would eventually settle down with. Joe was quiet, reserved, very smart, loved running and triathlons and apparently liked me as well. Things moved along and we were married in the late spring of 2009. I had met the man of my dreams. He shared my interests, he loved me with all my flaws, and he was my knight in shining armor, always there to shield and protect me. Before we knew it we were expecting. While marriage and the birth of our first child had changed everything, I still had my sights set on finishing what I started and fulfilling my dreams of becoming a physical therapist.

When the program inevitably discovered I was pregnant in the summer of 2009, the director called me into his office again and congratulated me on the baby on the way. Mark wished me luck in all my future endeavors and thanked me for my time in the program. No one expected me to continue a doctoral program pregnant or with a brand new baby at home, especially with my medical history that had already derailed my first year in the program. When the director found I had no intentions of quitting now, he was excited and again developed an alternative program to keep my skills honed while I was at home with the new baby. I would still start back with the fall class of 2009.

Repeating the semester from the fall of 2008 meant I was taking the same classes I had left in the middle of the semester the year before. With the baby due in the middle of the semester, I would again miss the same material. Professors Dave, Elaine, Dennis, and Nancy bent over backwards and flipped the order of the material taught in their respective classes. I was shocked and grateful they would do this just for me. All I had to do now was study and prepare for the baby.

Apparently, when I have any type of medical condition, whether it be my knees, my mind, or now my pregnancies; my body likes to challenge all the medical experts and literature. This time I developed atypical symptoms for a very rare condition known as HELLP syndrome (.001% of all pregnancies). HELLP is a life-threatening condition that can lead to a mortality rate as high as 25% for the mother. My atypical symptoms for this rare condition consisted of uncontrollable back pain, headaches, and nausea and vomiting during the 34th week of pregnancy that ultimately brought me into the ER where I was diagnosed with a chest cold and told my back pain was to be expected. I overheard the jokes the radiology techs were making about my complaints and that further led me to never complain again until my 36 week checkup, by which time my urine was brown (early signs of liver failure). Once my symptoms were correctly identified, I was admitted for an emergency C-section. The doctor informed Joe and I before they took me back that the baby was fine but he couldn't be sure about me, and Joe needed to call someone to be with him. Furthermore, Joe was not allowed back to the operating room where the anesthesiologist was screaming at the doctor to wait until I was asleep before she made her first cut.

After my three day stay under 24/7 intensive care observation and two additional days on the regular maternity ward, we were discharged home with a healthy baby. My recovery took a little longer than expected, but I was back to school within 10 days of the birth of our first son, Jackson.

I was married, with a new baby. I made it through a whole year, 2009, without an episode. I had a good partner committed to me, our family, and my health. Everyone, including my doctors, believed this might finally be the turning point in my episodes. My mind had not frozen during all this stress and I was able to bypass the most difficult time of motherhood, the time most mothers have problems; postpartum depression. I thrived and sailed through those early months, unscathed. Given that we still didn't know the trigger of my episodes, we all assumed it must have been associated with stress. Why some stressful events seemed to affect me more than others that were just as life-altering, we never could understand. We simply hoped I had finally turned a corner - finally beaten the invisible wounds.

But the episodes returned the next year, and the next, and the next. Over the course of 11 years since my first episode, I was 'locked-in' nine times. Nine times I lost all ability to function. The episodes would last anywhere from two days to three months. I could never seem to get away from them, no matter how hard I tried or how many new and different treatments and medications I took to prevent them. While each episode seemed to become less severe, they also seemed to last longer. My family, friends, doctors, and I explored all possible "triggers". Was it the stress in my life, or discrete events that would lead me to the next episode? The only pattern that seemed evident during all but the 1st episode was that they seemed to happen during the months of Sep, Oct, Nov, and Dec. There was a noticeable pattern emerging. They appeared to be seasonal. But I was not in this battle alone.

If I have learned anything through all these episodes, it's the value of those you surround yourself with. The strength and dedication of those around me cannot go unnoticed.

My hero and partner in crime, Joseph Furdek. Truly the best partner I could have ever asked for.

Photo courtesy of Marcia Seiler

Our boys, Jackson & Henry

18

MY TELEPHONE TREE

2005 TO PRESENT

During every single one of these episodes, my friends and family have always rallied around me. I could not tell this story without mentioning what others have done for me and how thankful I am. These people have come to my side to support me each time, even my coworkers and neighbors with whom I have chosen to share my struggles. I now openly share my symptoms and fears with others close to me. I want them to be aware of what happens to me when I suddenly appear different, no longer my happy-go-lucky self; 'locked-in', and quietly paranoid. I often worried about the stigma that can sometimes accompany mental illness. I worry moms might not allow their children to play with mine or allow their kids to visit my home. I want them to understand I am not a threat or person to be feared. I do not become the monster that sometimes Hollywood portrays of people with a mental illness. I do not lash out in anger or hit another person. If anything, I withdraw and need the comfort of family and my home.

I need others to know my now well-rehearsed and used support plan. Joe is always contacted first, and he immediately drops everything so he can be by my side. His bosses, coworkers and secretaries quickly cover for him and rearrange his schedule so he can spend the next few days/weeks at my side as much as his family medical leave allows. My doctors are called and my family is notified of my condition. Everyone quickly assumes the roles needed to make me feel safe and keep me from going into the psych ward.

I always thought of myself as very lucky to have my family and friends' unwavering support during these times (most do not). When I returned home from the combat zones after the first episodes, my friends Heidi, Jen and Kiri would open their homes to me for up to months at a time as I worked to get my possessions out of storage or find a new place to live. They would comfort and cheer me on as I struggled to get back up on my feet each time, and I could not have done that without them. Old high school swim team mates Elizabeth and Alex, whom I had not seen in years and suddenly found myself with at a swim meet I was observing in DC at the start of an episode, carefully took me aside, listened to my fears and ensured I traveled home safely.

My uncle Bob used to pick me up at my grandmothers and drive me to my medical appointments around town. He would take me out to his farm and plant trees on his land in honor of my fallen comrades and friends as a way to help me heal. He would drag me out of my bed when I wanted to hide at my grandmother's house. Bob made me run errands with him around town, just to get me to integrate back into crowds and be around people again. My Aunt, Phyllis, wanted to help me find a husband and start a family. She planted a statue in my grandmother's yard in honor of Saint Joe and asked that he send me a man. Now I have a Joe. Another set of aunts and uncles, Helen and David, would drop everything and come to the ER to relieve my friend, stay at my grandmother's with me to help both of us when I could no longer function, and just stay at my side through good and bad times until my parents could arrive. Upon my return home, the Dawn Chasers would rally around me each time and pull me outside in the early morning hours for runs, watching the beauty of the sun rise on a new day.

My family and friends' commitment to my health and well-being was unbreakable. My brothers Ben and Josh, sisters Marney and Abigail, and friends across the country would call and check on me all of the time. My girlfriends, Laura and Karin, used to come by and hang out with me, putting me to work on mindless tasks. I was grateful they got me off the couch when I was afraid to leave my house.

One of the bridesmaids at my wedding and a lifelong Academy friend, Jess, always called during my episodes to check on me (even the first one once I arrived at the Army Medical Center in DC). Another bridesmaid, Alicia, was in the running group and tried to visit and comfort me while I was in the hospital. And the final one was my classmate Jill who took me to the ER, and stayed by my side until I was safe with medical personnel and family. My father rushed up each hospital admission and sat by my side in the family rooms talking to me. My mother would call every day the hospital would allow. She sent her best friends to sit by my side until she could visit. She would then take me home when her work schedule would allow. My bosses and professors in every town, in every job, were always accommodating. They kept me on staff, giving me second and third chances. They continued to give me a paycheck when I was salaried as I pulled myself together and got back on my feet. Most employers and school programs, given the circumstances and the uncertainty of my condition, would have understandably shown me the door.

During the episodes, I would yearn for my grandmother's company and often just hang out at her house, working in her garden or sharing a glass of wine to pass the time. I visited my grandmother on a regular basis after marrying Joe. I would bring my children to her home to play, talk and just enjoy her company. My grandmother would always tell me the only thing she held against Joe was he took her roommate away, but that if she had been a few years younger, she would be competing for Joe's attention as well. In my times of crisis, being in her presence always brought me comfort and peace. My grandmother always had a way of making every person feel good. She never focused or dwelled on herself but rather turning her attention, worry and concern towards others. When asked her secret of living a long life, she would always say "put one foot in front of the other and enjoy each and every day". During the time I lived with her and all the way up to her final weeks of life, she and I completed a recording we secretly worked on together for over eight years. The final product consisted of a series of questions about life and her advice that she answered, all asked by my six year-old son. Her answers were priceless and offer not only wisdom and grace, but capture the true loss of her soul on this earth. My grandmother, ever so gracious and humble, watching me suffer in silence always told me she wished she could take my place and set my mind free. Having lost her in the spring of 2016, if there was anyone in the world I would want to sit and share this story with the most it would be her. Perhaps she had a hand in leading me to a cure.

19

SEARCHING FOR A SOLUTION

2005 -2015

In the beginning, the doctors would always ask me to voluntarily check myself into the hospital, not because I was a suicide risk or a risk to harm others but I just froze and could no longer function safely in society. They wanted to keep a close eye on me as I tried new medications they hoped would cure me each time. They wanted to study and observe me more when I was in this state (I was always a mystery to them), and they wanted to keep me safe (everyone did). I meticulously saved every document, letters from friends describing what they observed during episodes, records of different medications trialed, hospital progress notes and medical records, and my own accounts and timelines of each episode in a folder that grew larger over the years. I would now bring this folder to every new doctor I consulted whether in the Army, VA, or civilian system. Each trip to the ER, I would bring this folder with me in hopes a new provider could understand the history and my past and maybe offer an appropriate diagnosis and treatment to free me from my wounds.

Now, since I married Joe, I have not checked back into a psych ward. I think somehow I know I am always safe with Joe. He is able to calm me down and reassure me each time. I HATE THE PSYCH WARD. I think it was one of the worst decisions the doctors and I made (four times I had to go in and traverse through seven different wards). I was fighting my own battles at the time. It seems they were only magnified with unwanted advances or encounters with angry or pitiful patients who would scream and throw couches or tables, fight with staff in the hallways as I tried to get some much needed sleep and recover. I was always miserable, fearful of the very place that was supposed to keep me safe. While a psych ward may be appropriate for some patients, the run down, dilapidated halls I found myself in each time never helped me heal.

As soon as I thought I had finally won and conquered my "episodes", my life would stop and I would again lose all control of my mind. Every year or two, my whole life screeched to a halt. I couldn't function. I couldn't workout. I couldn't watch TV. I couldn't work. I couldn't finish a single task I had mindlessly performed the week before, including picking out the clothes I would wear for the day. The only exception was somehow I was on automatic pilot taking care of two little boys by the summer of 2013, Jackson and Henry. During each episode, I would sit in a corner of the house staring at the ceiling throughout the day. Even though eventually I would sleep soundly, I was afraid to close my eyes at night. I dreaded the mornings, wishing I was dreaming...only to awake to another day filled with paranoia and fear. As the weeks and months dragged on, Joe would return to work and my days consisted of getting the boys off to daycare and school and sitting and waiting for Joe and the boys to come home. I was afraid to even go to the store myself. I was afraid to move. I was afraid to talk to people except my mom, dad, Joe and a professor I called endlessly for comfort but would always reassure me these recoveries take time. I actually loathed talking to people. I was afraid to go out in public fearing the shame of what others must be thinking of me. Each time, all the memories of the war came flooding back. I was back in the valley, lost and confused. And no doctor in the Army, VA, or civilian profession could figure out how to fix it. My family and I sought opinions of a lot of doctors, both military and civilian, across the country over the years. They would always resort back to one of the eleven diagnoses that were either not true or I could never relate to in the literature and research. Again, I didn't think the medicine they prescribed even helped because the fears always came back, haunted me while I took the very medicine meant to stop my symptoms. My doctors would tell me some of these symptoms they saw in me they had also seen with men returning from the war but their episodes were always coupled with rage and violent outbreaks or suicidal thoughts. I was never like that. I never wanted to take my own life or hurt another human being. I love life too much for that. Normally the doctors would resort to the Bipolar diagnosis because it most closely matched some of my symptoms. However, I felt the diagnosis never met the criteria of what was written in the literature. Anyone who knew me well, knew 95% of the year I was a high-functioning, multi-tasking wife and mother, juggling a career, children, multiple house renovations, and my own athletic endeavors. I could accomplish almost any task with ease. I was cool, calm, collective, happy, loved life and my family and friends. I never seemed depressed to anyone else, especially to myself! My friends who had known me for a long time already discounted the Bipolar diagnosis, as they knew the definition, with extreme highs and extreme lows known to come and go throughout the year. Eventually the doctors and the therapists who spent years with me, having seen me in their office 95% of the year feeling perfectly fine and functioning, would come to the same conclusions, Bipolar as defined in the literature, was not my correct diagnosis.

Over the years I was the subject of medical school lectures and case studies. They put me in front of panels of experts and always asked me the same questions again and again, reverting back to diagnoses they were familiar with in the American DSM. It was finally to the point, with the type of questions they asked, I knew before they told me what they thought my diagnosis was at the time. I heard it so many times I could predict their opinions. I spent my own money in the civilian sector hoping for a new treatment, research, or a diagnosis. Three long deployments in four years had taken its toll so long ago. Now I wasn't even able to function in the civilian world, in a completely different career, with a wonderful family 5, 7, 10 years down the road. The "trigger" each time was never the same as the last.

One well-meaning counselor, hoping to ease the stress, said I just needed to go home and live as a housewife, raise my children, clean the house, cook the food, and support my husband. I always wanted more- staying at home wasn't for me. A professor at school completely dismissed this career suggestion from the professional and rallied her colleagues and my classmates to further help and cheer me on across the finish line. PT school was put on hold three times for me while I was in the program due to episodes and other health concerns. I finally graduated and earned my Doctorate in Physical Therapy and passed my licensure boards for the profession 6.5 years after I decided to go back to school. Each time I had an episode, the VA's vocational rehab program with counselors, determined to see me succeed, continued to pay my tuition and tutoring. Friends, professors, and classmates would rework schedules and plans to help me stick it out.

I had many providers over the years. One doctor in the VA, who is a well-respected professional in town, followed my case for almost four years. His ultimate conclusion surmised they would probably never know in my lifetime what was ailing me. Clearly I was devastated.

Perhaps my favorite provider to date and one of the most dedicated professionals I have ever worked with is a nurse practitioner named Tammy. Tammy, like other mental health providers in the VA's system, managed a caseload of patients meant for probably four or five providers. When she first met me, she had mounds of paperwork and medical history notes over the previous nine years of my life in the mental health system. No civilian professional or overloaded doctor at the VA had the time to peruse and completely grasp my complicated history. She quickly realized every time I would have an episode it was less severe, but it would last longer than the previous one.

Working with Tammy, we were able to recognize and pinpoint symptoms that surfaced when an episode was imminent. Over a period of hours or days, triggered by an often inconsequential event, no more stressful sometimes than making a wrong turn, I would start to lose my confidence. I would fight it as best I could. Tammy quickly caught on to the seasonal factor of my episodes, and she would start ramping up my medication dosage during the most frequent time of the year that my episodes seemed to occur. Along with the increased dosage, she had anxiety medication ready just in case. Joe could easily see when an episode was setting in. I would come home and he could tell I was different. Joe would try to calm me down and help me snap out of it, but it hardly worked. I would eventually lose sleep that night and then I would start the next day 'locked-in', not looking forward to what seemed like months to return to my normal state of mind and function. Each day during these episodes, I would look at him and say I wish I wasn't like this. I'm going to try something new and different today and try to snap out of it. When he returned at the end of the day, he would find me helplessly sitting on the couch, lost. He would always hug me tight and say hang in there, you will get better. Each time I would get in that state of mind, time and time again, I would think I would NEVER get out of it...I would be 'locked-in' forever.

It got to the point, Joe and I would put together a plan for the next one. Work schedules would be rearranged, budgets adjusted for missed work days, vacations would be rescheduled all in an effort to prepare for the next episode. I never took a full time job as a PT for fear of the time missed when I would have an episode. Rather, I worked PRN (as needed), easily canceled with low census in the hospitals but just as easy for me to make my own schedules or miss weeks at a time if needed to support my health problems. My bosses understood everything and wanted me to succeed. They quickly took me out of work schedules but made sure I stayed current on all of my credentials. I'm forever grateful for the opportunities they provided me and patience they had with my unorthodox situation and recovery.

And yet, every time I had an episode, without rhyme or reason, I would suddenly snap out of it. I remember the end of one of my last episodes; it had lasted a little over three months (the longest episode to date). It was a little after 11pm on New Year's Eve of 2014. I was sitting on the couch watching the festivities with my son Jackson, waiting for the ball to drop. I was dreading the upcoming visit to family for the holidays, avoiding preparations, packing, etc. I really didn't like being around a lot of people during these episodes and this one had lasted the longest.

As quickly as my symptoms had come on, they suddenly disappeared, just as every other episode had proven to do over the course of my medical condition. Suddenly, as I sat with my son in my lap, my mind relaxed. One minute there was dread and the next I was fine. The light switch had flipped again. My fears and paranoia were gone. I was excited to go see my family, excited to start the new year, excited to go pack all our clothes, and excited to wake Joe and tell him I was back to normal. I and everyone else eventually came to the realization that this was going to be something I would struggle with for the rest of my life. There seemed to be no end.

20

'UN-LOCKED'

2015 / LOUISVILLE, KY

It was the summer of 2015. Tammy and I were planning for the next episode we both knew was sure to occur. On this particular visit, she planned to increase the dosage of current medications and add a few medications that would be available to me once I found myself inevitably 'locked-in'. For the last five years my diagnosis had been Psychosis NOS (not otherwise specified). She was eager to help find a more permanent solution and stop my episodes. Tammy never stopped looking for an answer.

She was late to our regularly scheduled appointment after lunch. Tammy was excited and talking very fast. She explained she had just returned from a fascinating lecture at the VA given by a very respected expert in the field, Dr. Rifatt El-Mallakh, about soldiers with combat-related stress and PTSD. She mentioned he even worked at the hospital where I was practicing as a physical therapist. She felt if there was anyone who could figure out the answer to my decades long struggle it was him. Given that he did not work at the VA, and the red tape required to get permission to share health information with him was lengthy, she mentioned that it would probably be easier and faster for me to reach out to him. So with her permission, I wrote a brief history of my episodes over the past decade on a single sheet of paper. My timeline showed when each episode occurred and the circumstances surrounding each one with a brief medical history. I dropped the letter off at his office on a Friday afternoon. That evening at 6:30pm my phone rang. I cautiously answered an unknown number. It was the doctor. The expert was excitedly speaking to me on the other end of the line. He quickly told me he knew what was going on. Dr. El-Mallakh gave me a diagnosis I had waited years to hear. He called it **Cycloid Psychosis.** Speaking to me as if I were his colleague, he explained the diagnosis was mostly followed and used in Europe and not well accepted here in the United States, at least not in the DSM. He told me his colleagues had been trying to bring it mainstream to the medical community in the US for some time now. Within three minutes he had captured my attention more than any other doctor I had ever seen or talked to in over 10 years. The best part was he told me my condition could be fixed. All it took was a simple anti-seizure medication. He said the medication I had been provided up until now was mostly reactive and not proactive. He further explained in his opinion when my first episode occurred, I had been so confused, so overwhelmed by a particular traumatic event or series of traumatic events the only way my mind knew how to cope and protect itself was to shut down, lock itself in. Once this happens it was easier to happen the next time and the next time. Just as easy as it was to happen again, with the help of anti-seizure medication, my mind would adapt and be able to prevent it again and again in the future. Everything suddenly made sense. Dr. El-Mallakh was describing my symptoms better than I could describe what was happening to me, what I lived through over the last decade. Given it was August and my episodes normally occurred in the fall, he asked me how soon I could call my own provider at the VA. "Tomorrow," I excitedly yelled. He gently reminded me tomorrow was Saturday. "Well Monday, Monday I would call my provider with his number". In fact, I told him, I would personally take a note over to her office as she often did not have time to check messages until the end of a busy day. He cautioned he did not want to tread on her turf or make her feel like he was stepping on her toes, as she was my primary mental health care provider. I reassured him that Tammy had suggested I speak with him about my case. Dr. El-Mallakh told me he would explain the diagnosis to her and the medication that could help me and she could take it from there.

After we hung up, I looked up the research and found just about every case, while not exact, described my circumstances better than any other diagnoses in the past. For once, I felt like someone understood what has been ailing me since May of 2005. I now had hope I could take back my life. Tammy later confided she was in awe that this well respected, humble, and busy doctor had actually taken the time out of his schedule to personally address my case. She and her coworkers respected him very much and looked to him as a mentor, frequent consultant, and leader in the field. She looked up the research and information herself, presented it to her peers who all agreed this unknown diagnosis was the best explanation of my case and that the anti-seizure medication was the best choice to help in my recovery. Tammy got permission for Dr. El-Mallakh's suggested treatment approach from her superiors. The medication was prescribed one week later. As I held the tiny pill in my hand in front of my husband that first night, we both marveled at how this little white pill might change my life forever; as well as the lives of the rest of my family.

21

MY SERENITY

TODAY /LOUISVILLE, KY

I really do hope that I have finally turned a corner. While I have had minor episodes since 2014 and starting this new medication in the summer of 2015, they have been less severe and much shorter lasting, just as Dr. El Mallakh had predicted. As time goes on, our hopes are they will finally come to pass. As the doctor mentioned before, just as the episodes became more frequent and longer lasting over the years, subsequently as this medication settles and my body begins to recover, the episodes will happen further and further apart and not last as long. I eagerly await the medical community's reaction to my case. I'm curious as to whether they will agree that this is the final diagnosis and the correct medicine. It certainly seems to be going in the right direction. I have never been able to completely explain (in detail) the struggles and events surrounding each episode to my health professionals. Hopefully, this story fills in the blanks. I hope it can offer more insight and a voice for those unable to explain their struggles to their families and providers.

I've had moments over the last year where I felt like I may be starting an episode but when I awake in the morning, after having slept soundly overnight, I'm still my normal self. To the medical community this may sound exaggerated or hopeful thinking, but sometimes it's almost as if I can actually feel the medication affecting my brain. It is a well-known fact that the medical community doesn't really know why or how most psychiatric drugs work. The best way I can explain what happens to me whenever the emotions, fears, sudden lack of confidence start to set in (which previously led to an episode) is almost like somewhere deep in my brain, perhaps in the thalamus, I can almost "feel" something happening; I nearly go numb. Whether it's a release provided by the medication, or the medication that has built up over time in my system somehow slows down and blocks the nerves and vessels in my brain; I feel an immediate sense of relief and peace. I don't know; I can only speculate, hope and wonder. I'll leave the science to the pharmacists, researchers, and doctors to discount or explain. When this happens, I go to sleep at night when I would have previously fretted and loathed the coming of the next day, but now awake in the morning as if nothing happened. And when I do unfortunately fall back into my paranoia and fear, the medication dosage is raised by my providers and I quickly return to my normal, high functioning self.

For the first time in years, I have been able to actually enjoy the fall, celebrate my sons birthdays, not fear Halloween, and enjoy the presence of my wonderful family and friends during Thanksgiving and Christmas. I yearned for over a decade to enjoy these again. I am now currently stable and finally soaking in new memories and traditions. It has been a difficult, challenging, yet rewarding 11 years since this journey began, and almost forty years since this thing called life began for me. What a ride it has been and what a ride I hope it will continue to be.

What I have learned over my short lifetime when I have been confronted with a sudden unexpected change in my life, is to get back on my feet each time and try not to feel sorry for myself. The rollercoaster changes in my career path (welcomed or not) from physician to helicopter pilot, to engineer, intelligence officer to an FBI agent, civilian engineer to a Physical Therapist; I have always accepted change as a challenge not meant to beat me down but to build my character, taking me to new adventures.

When I tore the Anterior Cruciate Ligament (ACL) in my knee at the age of 11, I had to have surgery, not once, not twice, but four times over the next ten years. Each time I was told I should take it easy. I should let go of my sporting dreams, I should choose another career path. I was told the arthritis that would set in my knees from the surgeries would sideline me from all sporting activities by the age of 30, unable to walk without assistance or run pain free again. But like other medical conditions in my life, I proved the doctors wrong. I went on from those injuries to not only join the Army, but I jumped out of airplanes, and rucked for miles with 100lb ruck sacks. I had a great swimming career lasting over 15 years and set records in a division 1 NCAA program that lasted for 16 years. I climbed glaciers in Switzerland and Chile, ran the beaches in Australia, and conquered four ironman's and two marathons on these knees.

During each episode, nine over the course of eleven years, with an unbelievable support network cheering me on, I was determined to get back up again, to get out of bed in the morning, to not let it beat me. I will not accept being labeled as permanently disabled. I can, despite the circumstances, be a valuable contributing member of society. I sought out help rather than let help come to me. I pursued every resource, every opportunity, and I never chose to give up. I want to do it all and live the life of my dreams. And now, at this time in my life, I am. And if all this changes tomorrow, if life throws me another curveball, pops my joyful bubble, I will throw it right back, put one foot in front of the other and make the most of every day.

I would like to make it very clear that I do not want to attack the hands that fed me. The medical profession and the mental health community have a very difficult job. These invisible wounds cannot be seen by fancy equipment or corrected with surgery. There are not many lab draws or MRI's out there that can find anything to diagnose a patient objectively. It is all very subjective and based on years studying and treating those with invisible wounds. The story the patient tells the doctors and the facts about events surrounding their needing medical intervention have to be analyzed and compared to known symptoms that show patterns in other patients who appear to suffer from the same condition. Medications prescribed for other physical diagnoses for heart conditions and seizures have been found to strangely curb psychotic and mental health symptoms and for the most part no one can really explain why.

I've also been told the psych wards are much more capable now of handling the soldiers coming back from combat, including women soldiers. The doctors tried to the best of their ability to support me and to help me try to heal my wounds at the time. Resources they have available to them can be very limited compared to new technologies meant to help people stand up and walk again on new artificial limbs. Tammy tried relentlessly since she met me to reach out to other colleagues in the field to discuss my case, to review and debate the medications I had been prescribed. She hopes to make all the current trials and new treatments more accessible to our service men and women, veterans, and the civilian population in general. My hope is my case can continue to open new doors, start more discussions, and ultimately bring another account, a viewpoint of the struggles that I and perhaps many other soldiers have faced.

A former colleague, who still serves in the military and now commands a Brigade level unit, believes this story needs to be told and needs to be heard by soldiers and families who suffer in silence, afraid to come forward. He also says the Army tries very hard to screen and support its soldiers before and after deployments. They are encouraged, and it is now very well respected and accepted, to reach out for help and talk about the horrors they have witnessed. They are not quick to discount soldiers who have seen so much more than I ever will. It does not carry the stigma I once thought it had, if it ever really did. As much effort that has been given to support every soldier returning from battle, there is still more work to be done. One former soldier with whom I served in Iraq and now works stateside with special operations soldiers states: "While there is a tremendous effort and investment in the total soldier fitness there is still a gap that has yet to be adequately addressed".

After reading my story, I hope the reader walks away with a more open mind to those who suffer from mental illness and sometimes find themselves in the confines of a psychiatric ward. Those secretly dealing with inward demons are everyday people too. Everyone struggles with something, whether visible or not. Everyone willingly or unwillingly chooses to let those struggles either rule their every waking moment or deal with them, accept them, get help and move on. The DSM that lacks my diagnosis has 100s and 100s of commonly known conditions that trap the mind and offers treatment plans that have helped others heal. Whether it be yourself or someone you know, seek out the help that is readily available in the community. My story is a testament to the fact that there are many who want to help those with a mental illness succeed. The professionals in the field of mental health are very respected, very well educated and very dedicated to their patient population.

To the doctor I have never met (except spoken to briefly during a 10 min conversation on the phone)[3]. To the doctor who has finally given me hope after 11 long years, I often look for you around the hospital or working with the patients in the psych ward. If by chance I happen to meet you face to face one random day in the hospital, I will probably drop everything, hug you and just sob. Thank you. Thank you for your dedication to your profession. Thank you for your willingness to consult patients and colleagues daily to find the best practice possible for each individual. Please continue to try in every way possible to make my case, the diagnosis and the treatment plan that is apparently well accepted in Europe, more mainstream and accepted in the US. Since the writing of my story, there have already been others identified by my provider and her peers who have benefited from your treatment approach. Considering the number of providers I have seen over the years, clearly there is a gap of knowledge with this diagnosis and use of the medication. Continue to lecture and debate with your students and colleagues about the uniqueness of this diagnosis and others. Your dedication to your profession has provided long sought answers for me and other professionals that could perhaps enlighten colleagues and others that are out there

---

[3] I finally did get to meet this doctor although it was not as dramatic a meeting as I thought would happen. He is just as excited to provide my story and the diagnosis to others. In the near future we will coauthor a case study on Cycloid Psychosis and the treatment plan in some medical journals.

lost and 'locked-in' or perplexed by the symptoms of their patient. I hope these efforts will help others who may struggle with the same symptoms that have chased me in my dreams and in my life since that fateful day in May of 2005.

Whew, it really does feel good to get all of that off my chest!

22

A PHYSICIAN'S PERSPECTIVE

DOCTOR RIFAAT EL-MALLAKH / CYCLOID PSYCHOSIS

Written by the physician who hopefully has closed the chapter on the mystery that has ailed me for over a decade.

The brain is the organ that we have that can look and assess a situation in a way that leads to being able to solve a problem. When a disease occurs that involves this organ, the patient loses the ability to take stock of what is happening or understand what is going on. This can be very scary, confusing, and disorienting.

That is what happens when people experience a psychosis. Psychosis is the medical term describing a brain that cannot tell what is real from what is not real. People who are psychotic will sometimes hear things that are not really there, but will actually believe that they are hearing something that is real. They may believe things that are not real. Their brains also simply make more errors, so things around them are misperceived and misunderstood. They may become very suspicious because people are telling them that these experiences and beliefs are not really happening. They can become distrustful, isolated, and confused.

With the brain so dysfunctional, it is difficult to get along in the world. People around the patient realize that they are ill, but have a very hard time knowing what to do to help. It is usually scary to interact with someone that made sense in the past, but is now confused, paranoid, or hallucinating. It is particularly frightening for everybody if this is happening on the battlefield!

There are many conditions that can cause psychosis. Most of these are chronic, meaning that the person becomes sick, and even if they get better, they are still sick. These include conditions like schizophrenia or dementia (like Alzheimer's). There are a few conditions where people can become psychotic and then totally recover. The most common of these is a physical illness (like high fever or confusion around a seizure), or bad reactions to drugs like amphetamine or heroin. Finally, there are conditions where a person gets very sick and psychotic, recovers, but may get sick again. These recurring diseases with full recovery generally involve the mood disorders – recurrent depression or bipolar illness. If the person is experiencing recurrent psychosis, without mood symptoms, and with full recovery between the episodes, then the condition is called cycloid psychosis.

Cycloid psychosis is a diagnosis that is not frequently made because it is not in the book that the American Psychiatric Association publishes that lists the recognized psychiatric disorders – the Diagnostic and Statistical Manual or DSM. It is not clear why cycloid psychosis is not included in this diagnostic book, but its absence means that new trainees may not learn about it. In countries that do not rely on this book as much as the United States and Canada, the diagnosis of cycloid psychosis is a bit more common. Frequently, when someone in the United States with cycloid psychosis sees a psychiatrist, they are given a diagnosis of unspecified psychosis.

It is not clear what causes cycloid psychosis, or why people get it. There seem to be a couple of characteristics that are important. The first episode tends to happen in the setting of a chronic, unremitting stress – a difficult situation that seems to have no end and is out of the patient's control. Ultimately, the patient gets treatment and the episode ends, usually within about 1 – 2 months of starting. However, once the first episode happens, it is easier for the brain to get sick again. This means that the severity or the chronicity of the stress in subsequent episodes, can be less than in the initial episode. The more episodes the patient has, the easier it is for the patient to get sick again in the future. This usually means that aggressive treatment early in the course of the illness improves the long term outcome. By the same token, if the recurrence of episodes is not stemmed early, the condition can spiral out of control with a lot of episodes and a poor outcome.

Treatment can be divided into two phases. The first is the acute phase, when a patient first develops the psychosis. Everybody agrees that antipsychotic medications must be used in this phase. These medicines work to control psychosis independent of the cause. Problems with misperception of reality tend to respond better than problems related to false beliefs or paranoia; but eventually most symptoms get better. The second phase focuses on recurrence prevention. But here there is less agreement on what needs to be done.

Some doctors see this as a primary psychotic illness and focus on using antipsychotic medication to prevent the future episodes. Others see this as a condition that is related to the mood disorders and utilize mood stabilizing medications to try and prevent future episodes. Some believe that it is best to address both potential causes and treat patients with both mood stabilizers and antipsychotics. There are now a lot of medicines to choose from, and patients can usually find a medication, or a set of medications, that are effective and well tolerated.

Prognosis depends on a several variables. The first is the number of episodes that have occurred. The smaller the number, the easier it is to prevent future episodes. In other words, the interventions are more effective early in the course of the illness, but may become less effective if the illness has persisted for a long time. The second has to do with the level of *perceived* stress. Remember that the patient gets sick because they are in a bad situation that seems to have no end. However, these variables are subjective. So, what seems to be bad today, may not seem too bad at some point in the future, or vice versa. Similarly, what seems to be endless or hopeless now, may be quite tolerable if viewed differently. These are the reasons that psychotherapy, or talk treatments, can be quite effective in preventing recurrence. Psychotherapy can reduce the levels of subjective stress and give the patient a sense of mastery of their lives. Psychotherapy also can help patients reframe things that they do not feel that they are helpless or things are hopeless. Finally, patients have to be careful to not fall victim to associated anxiety. These experiences are so powerful and overwhelming, that it is easy to become scared of things that previously were not scary. It is easy to think that avoiding things is what needs to be done to prevent recurrence. It is easy to decide that limiting life's experiences and challenges is what needs to happen to avoid future episodes. This creates an anxiety that ends up being more harmful and more limiting than the actual biology of the illness. Psychotherapy is generally very helpful in avoiding this pitfall.

Doctor El-Mallakh's proposal to the
American Journal of Psychiatry after reading my book:

We would like to propose a Treatment in Psychiatry article that explores the diagnosis and treatment of cycloid psychosis. This diagnosis has been described in the literature, and can be seen as an extension of bipolar illness without the mood symptoms. It is not widely recognized, and our case highlights the problems associated with lack of recognition and delay with adequate treatment. We believe this would be an important contribution to aid practicing psychiatrists. Please let us know if you require additional information or a sample section of the paper.

And the response from the editor:

Thank you for your interest in the American Journal of Psychiatry. We would be happy to receive your Treatment in Psychiatry paper for review, but please note that papers proposing new diagnostic terms are difficult to write and often do not fare well in review. In this case you are drawing attention to an older diagnostic term - and it will be important to discuss, in the context of your clinical case, how the clinical syndrome fits with current diagnostic classification in the DSM.

Sounds like a challenge but I have no doubt Dr. El-Mallakh is the best professional to submit this recommendation.

CAROLYN FURDEK

23

AFTER ACTION REVIEW

The Civilian Psychiatric System

You've read my experiences in the psychiatric system. Here is a quick reference to the path most civilians would take today in a psychiatric crisis:

Patients deemed not at risk for threatening themselves or others participate in group and one on one counseling with mental health providers. They are monitored by a treatment team (psychiatrist, psychologist, registered nurse, social worker) for further care and compliance

Patients deemed at risk to harm and unwilling to voluntarily enter a psychiatric ward are placed into Emergency Protective Services by the Police, their providers, their family or friends. A patient then receives acute medication, a treatment team to manage their case, and 24/7 observation in a psychiatric ward at a local hospital for normally anywhere from a 72 hour hold to as long as two weeks. Sometimes patients can stay under court order for months.

If placement is available once they are stabilized they are transferred to either a private facility covered by insurance or private pay. If indigent they are transferred to a state institution for subacute care. Some are deemed stable enough after acute hospitalization to return home with the care of a family or friend responsible for their well-being with 24/7 supervision.

Once found to be stable enough to return to the community from subacute care they can either return home again in the care of family or friends or possibly have placement in a halfway house to slowly transition with resources available to assist in their reintegration to society. A select few have serious criminal charges pending at discharge and are transferred to jail.

Sometimes the saddest patients I treat on the psych wards are the Alzheimer's or dementia patients, often frail and elderly, no longer in their right frame of mind, not always a dangerous threat to others but now share a room with or sit at tables with the enraged irritated patients who throw chairs and fight with staff, until placement can be found. According to care coordinators and providers, normally the hardest patients to find placement for are the older population nearing the end of life. With time spent on a psychiatric ward, these types of patients are deemed a high liability for a nursing home or other long term care facility.

On a good note, trauma based care is gaining momentum with the treatment teams and providers. This care is centered around the trauma that led to the mental health problems and coping skills that some patients have developed. For instance, a 20 year old adult who was sexually and physically abused throughout their childhood often lack coping skills that allow them to be productive members of society. The teams therefore, focus their resources and treatments with individualized care meant to support each unique need for a successful recovery process.

Most providers in the United States point out the stark differences, public acceptance and resources available for the psychiatric community in Europe compared to services on American soil. Television and radio commercials supporting mental health are played not weekly but hourly in Europe, and public figureheads such as Princess Kate, actors and sports figures support and encourage assistance for those struggling. This regular show of support has led the European community to accept mental illness as more common than not among their friends and neighbors, leading to increased sympathy and less fear.

Unfortunately, in America most of the severe mentally ill fall through a revolving door. They are in and out of the wards every couple of months. Many are homeless with no family to support them, battling alcohol or prescription/illegal drug abuse used to numb the pain from old injuries, poor choices, or hide from nightmares they can't control. Or they hide at home trying to hold a job perhaps in the cubicle next to you, out in the community with little help quietly suffering. Sometimes they reach out, sometimes they run out of money for their medications keeping them stable, and sometimes they just push all help away. But most continue to go in and out of the wards and institutions for the rest of their lives.

If YOU feel so inclined, be the voice of change, and an advocate for those who can't speak for themselves in your Community!

Suggestions for Improvements:

I am a firm believer if you find fault in a system or process you should always have suggestions or recommendations to improve the situation or process

The psych ward of tomorrow

- If I had deep pockets and all the money in the world to donate to my local mental health community or eager donors ready to tackle this situation, this is what I would envision for the psych ward on the grounds of the hospitals for tomorrow.
- Community/hospital based group homes vs institutional wards, with up to 8 to 10 people with similar diagnoses living in more of a home like setting with single bedrooms. With as much of the home amenities that would safely be allowed. Cloth vs vinyl couches, colorful comforter's vs hospital sheets, restaurant tables and safe kitchens for eating. Much like the cancer floors in hospitals with carpet and single rooms, beautiful art and pictures on the walls.
- Women placed in separate quarters from men. I often see male patients are more prone to violence vs. women who are often reserved or scared. These women often get caught in the middle of a violent outburst by the upset male patient. Many patients are not in control of their emotions as they sit in their altered reality and it does not set anyone up for success if you mix them all together. These patients are all undergoing their own battles but each react in different ways.
- Home-cooked meals vs. hospital food. A local chef in our community, tired of running a restaurant and nearing the end of his retirement, now gives back to the local orphanage, fixing 5 star, delicious food for the orphans.

- Civilian clothes vs. hospital gowns. Or maybe just a comfortable set of pajamas
- Less group meetings between therapy sessions and more one on one mentors (not from the health community) that can share their own successes on returning to civilian life
- Flowers and plants allowed from families if deemed safe. Private gardens.
- Recreation rooms/gyms, patios, and walking paths away from the public but safe for the patients. Definitely not surrounded by concertina wire making a person feel more like a prisoner vs a patient. Exercise afforded with gym equipment is a great way to produce natural endorphins that can make one feel better.
- More phones allowed to call home/friends in a private room vs. a central phone where you have to stand in a hallway surrounded by 40 other patients listening in on your private conversations with family and only five minutes to talk.
- More trials outside the confines of wards to get out and ready patients to reintegrate back into the community with supervision.
- Resources for schooling and jobs available for soldiers, families, and the mental health community working with patients before they get out, vs. pamphlets or survey type phone calls once they get home. These resources could be held on the ward or provided as they walk out the door. Give them hope that things do get better.
- Provide private counseling rooms and staff offices.
- Soft music playing around the home, music therapy, sensory rooms and less fluorescent lights.
- More visits from family/friends if this is not the patient's reason for being in the ward. Even USO visits for military patients once individual patients concerned over privacy approve. Allow a family member to stay at the bedside all

day long and night as they can do in every other patient's room on every other unit in a hospital. Sometimes as a patient in a hospital you need an advocate for yourself and family members/friends are sometimes the best at doing this.

Research and examples of home like decor used in psych wards.

https://www.healthdesign.org/knowledge-repository/effects-different-interior-decorations-seclusion-area-psychiatric-acute-ward

http://www.wardipedia.org/69-therapeutic-interior-design-1/
(Permission granted from wardipedia who said they would be delighted if this author, and anyone reading the book, used their website as examples of designs of wards that have proven successful in Europe. They also suggested there are more examples of how to use these designs on another website: www.starwards.org.uk. *Permission also granted from Starwards to include their site.)*

I realize that most of these suggestions may have already been tried and perhaps deemed unsafe. But, I believe if services like these could be provided in a safe manner (and most have been effective in other wards) it could help patients feel like they are closer to home rather than closer to prison. Others would argue that there are programs set up like this after patients get out of the acute hospital psych wards but I would rather see something like this setting used from the very start. I think if I had come home to a place like this to heal for my safety yet still be monitored hourly by health professionals I would have perhaps done much better and less afraid or resistant to the help I was provided.

The stark differences in just the decor from the psych wards I've been on compared to the cancer wards on the same floor of the hospitals are surreal and sad. Thankfully, some hospitals are beginning to take notice and changes are being made, but we still have a long way to go. An average stay on a ward can be at least two weeks if not longer. I once spent 5 weeks on a psych ward waiting to be deemed sane but mostly waiting for a flight home. I believe time spent suffering on the wards in which I was placed, is worth every penny to make change.

I ask military post commanders and hospital directors in the public sector, even people in their own community who want to help, to visit your local hospital and observe the differences or similarities between the psych wards and the other floors of the hospital. Ask hard questions and challenge the staff, engineers, designers, and potential donors to make the wards at least equal to their other floors. Let's think outside of the box to design furniture and decor that is both safe for the patients but pleasing to the eye and comfortable to the patient.

While not trying to downplay any type of life-threatening diagnosis, who is to say that the cancer patient or the stroke patient should have better treatment, more funds, research, and donations given to support a cure. Why should they have better decor and furnishings to sleep in and pass their time in the hospital for their care than the patients who suffer from invisible wounds. The mentally-ill patient is suffering and drowning in their own hell, unable to see a way out, unable to move on or escape their nightmares, and in some cases see their only way out is to either drown their pain and struggles with addictions like drugs and alcohol or take their own life. Why should they not receive the same level of care, comfortable surroundings, and have the same opportunities for a cure or peace as any other patient suffering from an illness?

For every professional that is doubtful of your symptoms or unable to help you, there are thousands that want to see you succeed and provide you with the best care possible. Your primary care provider can always recommend you to a specialist. And there are always telephone numbers to call and people on the other end of the line that will listen and really do want to help.

Also, be aware that I am now ten years removed from my time in the service and eight years removed from my time as a patient in the psych wards. This story was not written to attack any of the organizations I have been a part of or the people who worked with me over the years. If anything, all the people I came in contact with, despite a select few, have gone above and beyond any expectations I or my family ever had to help me, in any way they could at the time and still do today. Things have changed for the better in the medical field, the Army, and the civilian world to give more attention to the mental health struggles of so many. Let's keep that momentum going.

Above all, actively participate in your care and surround yourself with people you trust. People who will help you make the best decision for you when you can't make it alone. Whether that be friends, family, or coworkers. Someone who will be there for you when you are home from the hospital, done with your medical appointment with your providers, or afraid to ask for help feeling as if you have nowhere to turn. And if you do not get a clear believable explanation of your mental struggles, then keep pressing, advocating for a different opinion and research.

CAROLYN FURDEK

24

THOSE THAT SERVE

As I said before, there are still soldiers deployed across the world, performing missions at night while we sleep in the safety and comfort of our beds. (It is not as readily covered as it was before, grabbing the headlines daily). I only deployed three times. I have friends who have completed dozens of deployments since 9/11. They are still in the military serving today. Packing their bags and kissing their families goodbye not knowing if they will return in one piece. Does anyone ever return the same? I know many of them struggle, yet they proudly continue to serve. They leave their families behind for months and years at a time for duty, honor, country and to protect the freedom and safety of their loved ones back home threatened by Terrorism.

I have learned, through my work at the VA, to cautiously approach the bedside of my Vietnam, WWII, and today's veterans in the hospital. Often times a loud noise or even gentle nudge of a patient sleeping with his back to you will cause them to awake in terror, screaming, and sometimes swinging at you in fear for their safety. I've heard numerous stories of soldiers that are afraid to go out in public every day. They are afraid to drive, constantly scanning the horizon for the enemy, fearful of trash in the road that might hide another deadly IED. They remember watching vehicles blow up in front or behind them as the soldiers inside them disintegrated before their eyes.

I never held the hand of my battle buddy as he begged for me or the medic to save him as he slipped away. Although I lost many dear friends, and soldiers I served with, I never lost someone so close that I couldn't breathe or bear to live another day. I never pulled the trigger of my weapon sending a bullet that actually found a human target, let alone an innocent bystander, a woman, a child, caught in the middle or used as a human shield. I never took the life of a fighter, a human being, no matter the unthinkable things he may have done to us. I never had to make the decision if it was him or me that would leave this world. Does anyone really know how they will act given those few microseconds when life and death decisions must be made. I hope given the circumstances I would have performed everything fearlessly and in good judgement without risking the lives of those around me. I was highly trained by the US Army, a good leader by all accounts and fearless. I was invincible. (Most of us had drilled so many times we could operate on automatic pilot effortlessly performing the motions to seize the objective safely.). I have great admiration for people doing this each day.

Sometimes I'm reminded of my own 'wounds' when for one reason or another I'm asked to provide a 2nd identification, usually my military retirement ID card that I use mostly for medical insurance purposes. Those with military backgrounds will often remark that I'm awfully young to be retired from the military. I'll quickly say I am medically retired and then they always look at me again searching for my missing leg or battle scars. I revert to an almost automatic response to these complete strangers and sheepishly say, "three deployments in four years can do a lot to a young mind". They almost always give me a sympathetic but understanding nod or handshake and thank me for my service. I always felt the American support for its sons and daughters is alive and well, in some ways perhaps more than ever.

Throughout all my deployments, potentially deadly situations, and countless close calls, I never felt ill-prepared. Even when I found myself in the middle of a dusty landing strip, in the unknown outskirts of Afghanistan; the Army, the Academy, my peers, sergeants, and commanders had given me tools, training, drills, tactics, and endless practice in order to keep myself and those around me ready and prepared. No one can predict the future or plan for every scenario for one to react in the face of danger, but I always felt the Army gave me the tools a soldier needs to adapt and make a good decision.

I know I was able to come through many stressful and potentially deadly situations during my previous two deployments without a problem. I did not lose my mind. I helped lead and got potentially deadly situations under control. Many have done the above things and done them with valor and selflessness. They have been given accolades and medals for their missions. I know many would give it all back to have the soldier back that lost his life, the one they couldn't save, safe at home with his family.

I see myself as the soldier back at the Army Medical Center in DC who survived the terrible blast that took the lives of four other men. I made it back home. However hard the circumstances, I survived to rejoin my family and live another day. I may not have run through a hail of bullets, or knocked down the doors of the enemy to root out the leaders wanting to defeat us. However, I saw more and experienced more than one probably should at 25 years old. Thank you to those that still wear the uniform today. Thank you for your sacrifice and your endless dedication to keep myself and my family safe.

CAROLYN FURDEK

25

TO THE AMERICAN PEOPLE

I cannot end this book without taking the time to mention the support I and others received while abroad and upon return home to American soil. I only heard and read stories from older soldiers about their return from Vietnam. I felt that Americans had done a complete 180 from their treatment of Vietnam soldiers in the 60's and 70's to the way they treated the next generations. Whether it was the thousands upon thousands of handwritten letters, pictures, care packages from school children, families, strangers across America and the world, support provided for our troops is undoubtedly humbling and one of the most grateful things I have ever taken away from the war efforts. Instead of angry hateful greetings with crowds who spit on you in uniform, there were parades in the streets and hundreds of people that would stand up and clap and cheer as we got off the airplanes and walked through the terminals of airports in our battle gear. It was not uncommon in airports to have strangers walk up to you and shake your hand, give you their first class seat on the airplane, cry with pride and thankfulness for our service. To the flight attendants on civilian flights that would serve us free drinks and bring pads of green grass from American soil to step on as we walked onto the airplanes to fly us into and out of country. Thank you.

To my mother and her friends, now 11 years after I left the combat zone, who still attend military parents and spousal support group meetings and send packages to my friends and former soldiers deployed, you are wonderful. To the random businessman who took me home from the airport to surprise my family and paid for a free meal for my grandmother and me upon my return. I've never forgotten your kindness. To the stranger who shook my hand, bought me a drink, and placed a $100 bill in my pocket. Thank you. To my father who would set a teddy bear with an American flag in front of his computer screen always open to a live video chat session when he rarely was not there to hold vigil at the computer waiting for me to randomly at any hour pop up online to chat. I love you.

To the thousands of prayer networks across all religions and beliefs, your thoughts, prayers, ceremonies, and tributes every day surely brought soldiers home safe to their families and hopefully comforted those who lost someone. To the Vietnam veterans who lead the front lines of America's support for its soldiers and new veterans, you deserved the same kindness upon your return but thank you for taking care of the younger generations. To the Patriot Guard (a motorcade of motorcycles) that make it their personal mission to attend every funeral for every soldier brought home from the battlefield and lead the hearse to the soldier's final resting place; your duty and dedication is unmatched. To the hundreds of soldier support programs that spend countless hours lobbying for veterans and soldier benefits, your dedication has not gone unnoticed. For the child who ran up to me at a baseball game to ask for my autograph, called me a hero and said she wanted to be a soldier when she grows up; please keep that belief of those who wear the uniform and share it with your friends. To the endless stream of USO guests, famous athletes and actors who bring us up on their stages in front of millions; thank you for the money you have donated, your time spent with us in the combat zone, the tears of appreciation shared with us is humbling. To the steakhouse that jumped at the chance to fly into the combat zone with your brave and willing staff to provide hundreds of thousands of soldiers deployed with a delicious steak and lobster for free. Bravo! To the mounds of free coffee, gym equipment, and electronics from home; Unbelievable!

To businesses across America that continue to provide free and discounted tickets, meals, and purchases for veterans, retirees, and active duty soldiers; we are forever grateful.

    To our leaders from the White House on down who tirelessly, away from the cameras, pen private letters and stand vigil at bedsides in hospitals and in the homes today trying to comfort and pray with the families of those injured or never coming home. Unforgettable. To the hundreds of hours and money spent by volunteers who gift to us toys for our children, plane tickets for spouses and families to visit the hospitals, quilts, clothes, snacks, houses and cars for the injured, your selflessness is invaluable. To the thousands of parents, teachers, and schoolchildren who send donated clothes per our requests for the locals or write letters or draw us all the wonderful cards and pictures; you make us proud to serve and protect you. When you are away from your family for so long, you have no idea how much your little 'note' means to the tired soldier in his or her bunk at night. The human spirit is alive and well across the American countryside. Thank you to all that have contributed in whatever way you could, and all that still do support the thousands of soldiers that are serving today away from their families in a foreign land.

*Again,
if this story can help just one person
it will have been worth it,
It will have served its purpose.*

----

*Remember, above all,
NEVER ~ GIVE ~ UP!*

Please feel free to share this story with others you think may benefit. But most importantly don't be afraid to tell your OWN... YOU can and WILL inspire others!

Thanks for reading this story to the end. Please pass it on!

Continue to follow **@lockedin2016** on Instagram or ***Locked In: A Soldier and Civilian's struggle with Invisible Wounds*** on Facebook for the latest updates, book signings, exciting changes and impacts this story appears to be encouraging across the soldier, civilian, and medical communities

REVIEWS

I could feel your thoughts and emotions as I read your story. I believe this will shine a light on so many men and women who have experienced the loss of control - MD

Just finished! Could not put it down!!! HN

Very powerful because I feel like you and I are just sitting down having coffee together as I read this. BE

It is really really good. I can say this, because this is not normally a book I would pick up and read. I am just a mom and a teacher and I bask in the freedom that I enjoy because of women and men, like you....It is wonderful work. It is fascinating and important to understand...I do not think there is a mother alive who would wish war on the people of the earth--but we are grateful for you who keep us safe and free. That said, war is what it is. It is heart wrenching and terrifying. I pray for the torments that haunt soldiers after the war ends. I hope that finding that voice might grant your mind and soul rest. - CD

I think it's an amazing story and am grateful you shared it with me...I do think it's an important story that you are sharing...it has the potential to help a lot of people. - LB

It was informative and educational but also so INSPIRING. I know your purpose was to focus on mental illness but what a great read for any young girl (or guy for that matter). - CV

All i can say is wow...I really think your story can help others who have been through the same thing. - BC

I genuinely appreciate the rawness. I didn't read anything that made me feel like you were not sincere with every word. I had my own struggles associated with that time in my life. While not the same, I felt ashamed...I didn't want to "share" my struggle. Reading your piece brought back a lot of emotions that I had opted to block out from that time in my life. Luckily I have had an awesome support system and I am at a better place in my life so "reliving" it through your stories was a bit cathartic. I find it incredibly brave of you to share your story. I have worked at U*** for about 5 years and my daily interactions are with the best of the best who have experienced the worst of the worst. While there is a tremendous effort and investment in the "total" Soldier fitness there is still a gap that has yet to be adequately addressed - JK

I read your story with interest, turning to compassion and ending with anger...your story should be required reading for the psychiatric community and the VA system. - HT

I hope that your story will bring forth a discussion on what we, as a society, expect from those who serve in the military and how our society should care and treat all those individuals. My hope is that many doors are opened through your sharing of such a personal experience. - ML

(With) B*** being gone all the time it ties into your intro...it took me a few times to get through it I kept getting choked up.....a roller coaster of emotions for me...our story needs to be shared. So many veterans suffer in silence because they do not want the stigma of being perceived as weak...Instead they medicate themselves with alcohol and drugs to suppress the images of war and multiple missions...I know I have PTSD from B*** many deployments and not being privilege to know where...in the world he has gone....will I see him again...when he comes home will he be okay...will he adjust to being home...I commend you for sharing your story with very intimate details...- GK

...I love hearing your voice in this, and the rawness of experience. - MK

I think that is an important story for both medical professionals and laypeople to understand the impacts of war, conflict, pressure to succeed and so much more can affect one's wellbeing. for doctors for diagnosing people and for other people to gain some compassion for those that have experienced hardship. and it doesn't have to be war per se, I could see this being important in battered spouse syndrome issues and other mental trauma (that can coincide with physical trauma). - AS

...the story is phenomenal, honest, and compelling. - SJ

What a powerful story of strength, resilience and recovery! Your story is a testament to the value of continuing to search for answers, even when you're being told there are none. Your symptom presentation is fascinating and I am so happy that you have found a treatment - KL

it's too often the wounds we don't see that are the most profound... - CF

You provide a voice for all of us who have struggled with or have known others who have struggled with mental health issues. You are a shining example to all when you advocated on behalf of those who couldn't fight for their own quality of life requirements. You are proof that it's ok to get mental health assistance and still live an amazing life doing the things you love. - SG

I started reading it today...I'm having a hard time putting it down... - CM

Amazing!!! I couldn't stop reading...I know your story will help many soldiers and others dealing with these symptoms and help to get it diagnosed correctly.... I am a school counselor now and the mental health needs of kids are not being met. I think the more we talk about mental health and share our struggles and successes we help the next generation. You are a brave soldier and fighter who didn't give up. - MC

Without going into detail, I understand and can relate. We all have our demons! There were several years after I retired that I was spiraling, I couldn't focus on things, and anxiety was crushing me, G**** and I were very close to divorce. As much as I didn't want to ask for help or admit that something was wrong, I knew that I didn't want to lose all that I loved. Bottom line, I got the help I needed. I learned how to cope and loose the anger and mind paralysis. - BK

I know it sounds cliché but if this helps even one person then it was worth your time and effort. - JK

This story will help so many veterans who have suffered and struggled in silence...and perhaps show them that asking for help is acceptable and is not a sign of weakness or reason for embarrassment. This story will also provide a comforting shared understanding for those who are currently undergoing treatment...what a relief to hear that this can happen to the best of us...even a successful, strong, and highly respected officer. - SG

I think it is fantastic that you are getting your story out there. There is so much of a negative stigma out there in the military. If your story can save just one person, you have done your job. - HW

My sister is in the mental health industry and she and her co-workers agree that every human has requirements for some kind of therapy. They regularly discuss their own issues with each other. It is perfectly acceptable to discuss in their workplace environment. Hearing this made me so glad she could talk through her problems with zero judgment. - SG

Surely this memoir will help others. You simply cannot be the only soldier who has had this happen. I would think that it has been happening to others for all of time. I would hope that it helps civilians not only to understand, but to help to diagnose and help civilians who might suffer the same type of symptom. - CD

I appreciate your raw honesty and think other readers will too...I admire your perseverance - EL

As a psychologist who teaches the DSM (begrudgingly), I think it's important that we don't allow diagnostic manuals and classification systems limit us, in our search for answers and treatment and I think your story is a testament to that. In terms of your suggestions about the psych ward: YES! There is currently a movement towards Trauma Informed Care, which includes many of the environmental changes, including interior design, that considers people's trauma histories. Your recommendations are spot on - KL

I think your recommendations are very insightful for the psych ward of tomorrow or should I say today . - SZ

I am proud to call you a former sister-in-arms and fellow graduate of USMA and fellow member of the first USMA cohort to graduate Navy Dive school - SG

God can work miracles out of bad situations. How exciting to see it unfold!! - TV

It is a beautifully written piece. I read it as soon as you sent it to me and read it again to D*** at his gravesite...Thrilled and at peace that you have embraced and disseminated your story in writing. May it comfort many others - GP

...it's great stuff, hopefully helping people with symptoms like you get the help they need - KM

...I had no idea any of that had happened and just the way you wrote it is a real eye-opener. - SH

I think it's so brave of you to put it down and courageous to attempt to help others - SD

Your story will undoubtedly help many of our service members, their families, and civilians alike....I can't wait to read it again. I couldn't put it down! - MN

Absolutely astounding. Your journey, drive and tenacity are remarkable. I feel certain this can help and give hope to countless warriors... Happy to have had the opportunity to serve with you. - SF

You were absolutely right to write it. If it helps a medical professional recognize symptoms like yours and make the right diagnosis for just one person, it would be invaluable. - SP

I am convinced that this will be a help to others who will go through something similar, or be a friend, leader, fellow soldier of someone who goes through something similar. I am so glad you chose to write this. – MH

I think it is important that people realize that individuals can have "a break" for a non-event like you did, and not just for a "failure" that ended up causing injury. One can easily imagine a person being overwhelmed by thoughts of doubt when something bad actually happens based on their actions or actions that they perceived to be their fault. but it can also happen z, when there is a non-event if the conditions are right. It is similar to "everyone" understanding that a soldier with a missing limb has been traumatized, but someone with PTSD may find it harder to point at the cause. That doesn't mean they don't have a serious problem.

On the flip side the amputee's overall trauma is bigger than the physical loss of the limb. The brain is a complicated thing. – AS

Sister I love you but I never want to hear of you peeing in a cup in the middle of the desert ever again -BH

Your story is compelling...! Moreover, it needs to be told! Very few accounts from women veterans are documented. Thank you for being courageous enough to unleash your narrative...This would make a great GI Film Fest documentary! JW

I'm a military brat and have many close military friends who have deployed multiple times to Afghanistan and Iraq. The topic can be so hush hush even in the military circles at times. I appreciate what you are doing for those who have not been able to speak about their own similar afflictions, for whatever reasons. By God's grace, this will continue to be a thing of the past for you and moving forward, you will change many lives by speaking your truth. – CM

CPSIA information can be obtained
at www.ICGtesting.com
Printed in the USA
LVHW081538150122
708671LV00024B/558